序　言

　　目前我國已有廿種產品，在世界市場佔有率名列第一。賺取外滙最多的出口貿易，實功不可沒，爲台灣經濟的支柱。因此，站在第一線的貿易商，更是台灣經濟躍昇的尖兵。當然我們不能以此現狀爲滿足，應該在日常實務上精益求精，開拓更寬更廣的境界。

　　「英文商業知識入門」全書共分十八章，包羅廣泛，從商務、信用查詢、報價、訂單、信用狀付款…到借貸關係、海上保險，並增列一般貿易書籍所沒有，但又非常必要的租船契約。每一章共分四個單元——實務解說、必備例句、貿易須知、模範書信，以最簡明的編排，使讀者達到最高的學習效果。

　　鑑於現代商業已從 telex（電傳）時代，漸漸移向以 word processor（文字處理機）爲基礎的 post-telex 時代，通信技巧越來越重要，本書乃滙集諸多

商用英文**必備例句**，提供最有效的英文表達方式；因為商業書信需要貿易實務的概念作基礎，所以每個單元開頭都附有**解說**，以闡明複雜難解的貿易實務；另外列有**貿易須知**，敍述各種重要用法、慣用語句等；並收錄精彩的**商業書信範文**，以俾讀者參考；書末附錄貿易英語略語一覽表，方便查對。

　　本書是商業人士、秘書、學生、自修者最有利的指導用書，若能熟讀本書，於日常業務必大有助益。

編者　謹識

目 錄

本書另有錄音帶四捲，由美籍電台播音員錄音，配合學習，效果更佳。

本書採用米色宏康護眼印書紙，版面清晰自然，不傷眼睛。

第1章
商務・信用查詢
Business Enquiry;
Credit Enquiry

　　詢問（enquiry）在貿易上通稱為「查詢」。包括交易第一步驟的索取目錄（catalog）、價目表（price list），以及詢問機種、性能、付款條件等其他交易內容。查詢越多表示生意越興隆。以下就來談談查詢函件的書寫要領：

　　1.　索取目錄及價目表是例行公事，因我方是買主的身分，over-polite、humble wording（過度客套、謙卑言詞）都是不必要的。通常用 Please send us the catalog and price list of your latest productions（or, products）. 就可以了。大可不必用 We beg you to send us the catalog and price list of your latest productions（or, products）. 這樣的句子，像 beg 這種字眼已經不用於商業英文了。

　　2.　除了 1.所說的之外，首次發出查詢函件時，還要寫明我方是如何知道對方的名字的，以及我方的 identity（身份）、business background 、交易貨品、數量及付款等。這是爲了先却除對方的不安，以期建立以後的交易關係。

3. 首次查詢函若以**訂貨折扣**(discount)或取得**銷售權**(**selling rights**)爲重點時，這已經不能算是查詢函而是某種 sales letter，所以必須寫明將來的發展、訂購數量的估計以及我方現在的狀況等等。

以上所提的既是查詢函件，當然也包括向第三者查詢欲交易對象**信用狀況**(credit status)的**信用查詢**(credit enquiry)。這是確定對方**財務狀況**(financial standing)、**信用**(creditability)及**交易方式**(mode of doing business)的極機密函件。無論是商務或信用查詢，只要是首次發信都應該以 salutation (問候)爲始，然後說明我方的營業和地位等等。第二次之後才可免掉這步手續。

商 務 · 信 用 查 詢 必 備 例 句

A. 商務查詢 (Business Enquiry)

a) 查詢目錄、價目表和最低價格

1. Please send us your catalog and price list of your *latest productions*.

請寄給本公司貴方的目錄和最新產品價目表。

2. Please let us have your prices *in sterling* for your latest productions.

請讓本公司擁有貴方最新產品的英鎊價格。

3. Kindly *quote us* your (lowest) prices for the goods listed below.

請報給本公司下列貨品的 (最低)價格。

➡ kindly 〔'kaɪndlɪ〕 *adv.* 請 (=*please*)

4. We should be pleased to receive
   your *illustrated catalog* and
   price list of Plastic Kitchen-
   ware.

本公司將很高興接到貴
方塑膠廚房用具的圖解
目錄和價目表。

➡ illustrated〔'ɪləstretɪd〕*adj.* 圖解的;有照片的

5. We should be glad to receive
   details of your prices.

本公司將很高興接到貴
方價格的詳情。

【說明】 price for～用於可變動的洽談價格,price of～則表不
可變動的固定價格,price on～用於對方所說的價錢。介系詞的
用法極其微妙,務請多加留心。quote 即 state the price of～
表報(價)或開(價)。

b) 首次照會信件

1. *Greetings* : *we are* one of the
   foremost textile traders in Taiwan
   mostly *engaged in* the export of
   textile products of all types,
   and having *a business background*
   of some 40 years.

敬啓者:本公司是台灣
一流紡織品貿易商之一,
主要從事各種紡織品的
出口,約有40年的商
務經歷。

➡ background〔'bæk,graʊnd〕*n.* 經歷;背景

2. Greetings : *ours* is a Hongkong-
   based import and export house
   dealing mostly *in* machinery and
   equipment of all types, and having a business background of
   some 30 years.

敬啓者:本行是一家在
香港頗有根基的進出口
商,主要經營各種機器
和設備,約有30年的
商務經歷。

3. Greetings : your name is already
   familiar to us, and permit us
   to write you to ask about the
   possibility of *opening an ac-*
   count with your house.

   敬啓者：久仰貴行大名，
   容本公司寫信詢問有關
   和貴行開啓商務關係的
   可能性。

4. Your name was given us by
   Messrs. AB & C.

   貴公司的名字是AB＆C
   公司提供我方的。

5. Messrs. AB & C has advised
   us to *get in touch with* you
   concerning....

   關於…，AB＆C公司
   建議本公司和貴方聯絡。

6. Messrs. AB & C have *recom-*
   mended you to us and we wish
   to know the details of....

   ➡ recommend〔,rɛkə'mɛnd〕 *v.* 推薦

   AB＆C公司推薦貴方給
   本公司，本公司想知道
   …的詳情。

7. *Through the courtesy of* Messrs.
   AB & C, your name has been
   supplied to us.

   AB＆C 公司好意提供
   貴方的名字給本公司。

8. *We are indebted* to Messrs. AB
   & C *for* your name.

   本公司深深感激AB＆C
   公司給本公司貴方的名字。

9. We hear that you are a *long-*
   established manufacturer of
   textiles of all types.

   本公司聽說貴方是歷史
   悠久的各類紡織品製造
   商。

10. The fame of your excellent products is well familiar to us, and we wish to *open*, if possible, *an account with you.*

久仰貴公司產品之優秀，如果可能，我方希望和貴公司開啓商務關係。

11. Your advertisement in August issue of the *Tradenews* interests us, and we should like to have full details of your offer.

貴方在貿易新聞八月版的廣告引起本公司的興趣，本公司很想擁有完整詳細的報價。

12. We have seen your newly developed product at ... and wish to *have from you a quotation on CIF Keelung basis*, together with more information on the same item.

我們在…已經看過貴公司新開發的產品，希望從貴公司得到一份到基隆運費、保費在內價爲基礎的報價單，和同一項目更多的資料。

13. Your newly developed product displayed at the Sydney Trade Fair has interested us and we should be very grateful to have a price catalog *thereof*, and *your lowest possible quotations CIF Keelung*.

本公司對貴方在雪梨商展所展出的新開發產品感到興趣，若能得到貴方的價目表，和貴方到基隆運費、保費在內可能的最低報價則不勝感激。

14. We learn from the China External Trade Development Council that you are producing *for ex-*

本公司從中華民國外貿協會得知，貴方以純獸皮和其它天然原料手工

port hand-made shoes and gloves in pure hide and other natural materials. There is a steady demand here for high-class goods of this type. Will you please send your catalog and full details of your *export prices* and terms of payment, together with *any samples you can let us have*.

製造皮鞋和手套出口。這裡對這類高級的產品有穩定的需求。煩請貴方寄來目錄、完整詳細的出口價格、付款的條件、和貴方能給本公司的任何樣品。

➡ hide〔haɪd〕*n.* 獸皮

15. We have seen your *advertisement in*... for your latest product COPYING MACHINE, and should like to have the details thereof.

本公司在…廣告上看到貴方的最新產品——影印機，因此想知道詳情。

16. May we ask you to *join in our business for a commission sale* of our products in the market of your locality?

本公司可以要求貴方加入本公司的商務，在貴方當地的市場代售本公司的產品嗎？

➡ commission〔kəˈmɪʃən〕*n.* 代辦

17. We should be glad to hear *at your earliest convenience* the terms and conditions on which you are prepared to supply.

本公司若能及早獲知貴方準備提供的條件則感幸甚。

18. Please *quote us for* the supply of the items listed on the enclosed *enquiry form*, giving your prices CIF SAN FRANCISCO.

請將列在附寄的查詢表中的供應項目，到舊金山的運費、保費在內價報價給本公司。

19. Will you please also state your *earliest delivery date*, your terms of payment, and discounts for regular purchases?

能請貴公司也說明貴公司最早的交貨日期、付款的條件、和定期購買的折扣嗎？

➡ discount〔ˈdɪskaʊnt〕*n.* 折扣

20. Will you please also send details of trade discounts and terms of payment? Are you prepared to grant special terms for an annual trade of £30,000 net?

能請貴方也寄來詳細的交易折扣和付款條件嗎？貴方準備答應每年交易額純利三萬英鎊的特殊條件嗎？

21. Please also let us know if you already have an *exclusive sales agent* or *distributors* for your products in the southern part of the US.

如果貴公司的產品在美國南部已經有獨家銷售代理商或經銷商，也請讓我方知道。

➡ exclusive agent 獨家代理商　　distributor〔dɪˈstrɪbjətɚ〕*n.* 經銷商

22. … we should like to discuss *the possibility of an agency* with you.

…本公司想和貴方討論代理權的可能性。

23. We should like to know if you
    are prepared to grant us a
    special discount.

本公司想知道貴方是否
準備答應給本公司特殊
的折扣。

24. We shall welcome an opportunity
    of discussing a *contract* with
    you.

本公司歡迎有機會和貴
方討論訂約事宜。

25. What would be your earliest
    delivery date?

貴公司最早的交貨日期
是什麼時候？

26. Would you be able to deliver
    within *five weeks of receipt*
    of order?

貴公司能在接到訂單五
星期內交貨嗎？

27. We should require the goods
    by June 1st at the latest.

本公司最遲在6月1日
前要貨。

28. Please advise us of your *freight
    rates*, Liverpool to New York
    for a shipment of ....

請告知本公司有關…從
利物浦到紐約的船運運
費。

    ➡ freight〔fret〕*n*. 運費

29. *Our bankers* are Bank of
    Taiwan, Taipei, to whom you
    may refer for our *financial
    and business standing*.

本公司的交易銀行是台
北的台灣銀行，貴方可
以向他們查詢本公司的
財務和營業狀況。

30. You can easily understand our *financial position* and *business integrity* by making reference to the A company.

貴方向A公司查詢，很容易就可以了解本公司的財務狀況和商業上的誠實。

➡ integrity〔ɪn'tɛgrətɪ〕*n.* 誠實；正直

【說明】 ① 29., 30.屬於「信用查詢」，在商務查詢信件中，爲了讓對方了解我方的狀況良好，常常要加上這一段。

② bankers ＝ 交易銀行

---

c) 非首次照會之信件

1. Would you kindly（May we ask you to）advise us of the details of your latest products？

能請貴方（本公司可以要求貴方）告知最新產品的詳情嗎？

2. We are writing immediately to ask you about the details of the services you could *render in connection with* the supply of newspapers and periodicals.

本公司立刻寫信詢問貴方可以提供的，有關報紙、期刊供應服務的詳情。

➡ periodical〔,pɪrɪ'adɪkḷ〕*n.* 期刊

3. We *hasten to* ask you to write us about a possibility of extending the term of the present contract by another 12 months, *viz*, until September of 1986.

本公司急著要求貴方寫信告知，有關現行契約期間延長 12 個月，亦即到 1986 年 9 月的可能性。

➡ viz 亦即；就是（拉丁語 videlicet 之略，通常讀爲 namely）

4. We hear that you have developed *a new pattern of* electronic type-writer, and should be glad to have full details.

聽說貴方已經開發一種新型的電子打字機，本公司將樂於獲知全部的細節。

5. Will you kindly send us samples of your *specialities* ?

能否請您寄給本公司貴方特製品的樣品呢？

6. We are *on the look-out for* the following items and should be grateful if you would send samples (specimens) of the same.

➡ specimen〔'spɛsəmən〕*n.* 樣品

本公司正需求下列各項目，若貴方能寄送其樣品，我方不勝感激。

7. We have a considerable *demand* here *for* ... and should welcome your pattern-book.

本地對…有相當大的需求，很歡迎貴方的樣品簿。

8. We are interested in your newly developed product and wish to *have from you* the details thereof.

本公司對貴方新開發的產品感到興趣，因此希望貴方提供其詳情。

d) 通用結尾用語

1. We look forward to hearing from you soon.

本公司期待貴方儘速回信。

2. We should appreciate a prompt reply.

若蒙迅速回覆，則不勝感激。

3. Your early reply would be appreciated.

對貴公司早日的答覆不勝感激。

4. Your *prompt attention to* this would be greatly appreciated.

若貴公司儘速辦理此事，則感幸甚。

B. 信用查詢（Credit Enquiry）

a）首次查詢

1. Greetings : we are export traders dealing in silk products, and are now planning to open account with Messrs. AB & C in your locality. Your name is already familiar to us, and we feel highly grateful if you will be *good enough to* advise us of the *credit status* of the said company.

敬啓者：本公司是經營絲織品的出口商，現在正計劃和貴地的AB&C公司開啓商務關係。我方已久仰貴公司大名，如果貴方能好意告知我方，上述公司的信用狀況，我方將非常感激。

2. *Through the courtesy of* China External Trade Development Council, your name has been supplied to us, and allow us to write you to ask about the

承蒙中華民國外貿協會的好意，提供貴方的名字給本公司，容本公司寫信問貴方，有關貴地AB & C 公司的信用狀

credit status of Messrs. AB &
C in your locality with which
we are now planning to *enter
into relations*.

➡ *enter into* 締結

況，本公司現在正計劃
和他們締結關係。

3. Greetings : we are indebted to
CETDC here for your name,
and allow us to write you to
ask about the *respectability and
standing* of Messrs. AB & C.

敬啓者：本公司非常感
激中華民國外貿協會提
供貴方的名字，容本公
司寫信給貴方，詢問有
關AB & C 公司的信用
程度和營業狀況。

4. Messrs. AB & C wish to *open
a credit account with us* and
referred us to you. We shall
be grateful if you will let us
know, *in confidence*, your
opinion of his financial standing.

➡ *in confidence* 秘密地

AB＆C公司希望和本公
司開啓信用關係，並請
本公司向貴方查詢。如
果貴方能秘密地告知，
您對其財務狀況的意見，
我方將不勝感激。

b）非首次查詢

1. We are writing immediately to
ask you about the credit status
of Messrs. AB & C *in your
locality*, with which we are
now planning to open account.

本公司立刻寫信問貴方
有關貴地AB＆C 公司
的信用狀況，本公司現
正在計劃和他們開啓商
務關係。

2. We hasten to ask you to write us about the creditability and financial standing of Messrs. AB & C....

本公司急著要求貴方寫信告知我方,關於AB&C公司的信用程度和財務狀況…。

3. We shall be much obliged if you will kindly give us any infor-mation respecting the reputa-tion, the **mode of doing business** and **financial resources** of Messrs. AB & C.

如果貴方能好意給本公司有關AB&C公司的商譽、交易方式和財力的資料,本公司將非常感激。

c) 回覆查詢

1. This company is **being pressed by** creditors and its position is **precarious**.

這家公司正受迫於債權人,狀況也不穩定。

➡ precarious〔prɪˈkɛrɪəs〕*adj*. 不穩定的

2. Executives of the company are inexperienced in the business and **extreme caution is advised in granting credits**.

這家公司的管理人員缺乏業務經驗,授信應非常當心。

3. This company is well-established and reliable.

這家公司有口皆碑又很可靠。

4. *The inquiree company* seems to have recently *embarked on* a rather risky speculative business just unfit for its *resources*.

您所查詢的公司最近似乎在從事一項與其財力不合，且相當有風險的投機事業。

➡ embark〔ɪm'bɑrk〕*v.* 從事　　speculative〔'spɛkjə,letɪv〕*adj.* 投機的

5. This information is strictly *confidential* and is given without responsibility on our part.

這份資料應嚴守秘密，本公司既經提出，本公司概不負責。

6. We trust that you will regard this communication as confidential.

相信貴方會將這次通信視為機密。

7. Some questionable rumour *is abroad with* that company.

關於那家公司有些可疑的謠言傳播著。

8. We regret the *unfavorable account* we have to make in reply to your enquiry of April 5.

答覆貴方4月5日的查詢，本公司很抱歉必須做不利的報告。

9. The information I have to *convey* you in reply to your enquiry of April 5 is unfortunately not such as you could desire.

答覆貴方4月5日的查詢，我必須通知貴方的消息，不幸並不如貴方所想的。

【說明】　8., 9.中所用的 have to 句型適用於結果並不理想的時候。

10. As this is the case, we deem
　　 it rather advisable for you to
　　 refrain from having relations
　　 with that company.

既然情況如此，本公司
認爲貴方避免和那家公
司有來往是相當明智的。

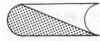 商務・信用查詢須知

1. 賺取外滙的方法

　　CIF　貿易上交易價格的代表，是從出口港到進口港的海上運費、保險費在內價（ cost，insurance，& freight ）。CIF San Francisco 就是指到舊金山的海上運費、保險費在內價。

　　這裏的 cost 是〔製造成本＋沿路裝卸費＋包裝費＋裝船雜費（包括搬運工資）＋檢查費＋利潤〕，以上這些費用即相當於FOB price（參照2），**因此CIF＝FOB＋I**（*insurance premium*）**＋F**（*freight*）。雖然在CIF條件中，負擔風險的責任於出口港完成裝貨時，就轉移到買方身上，但是貨物的所有權，則必須等銀行把裝運文件交給買方時才轉移到買方身上。在進口港之前的 cost、insurance & freight 由賣方先付，再以此交換船公司的提單（Bill of Lading－B/L）。而買方則以外幣付清這些款項，是賺取外滙的方法。

2. 節約外滙的一種方法

　　FOB　這是與 CIF 並列的貿易交易價格代表。正如前面所述，它是指到出口港裝船爲止的一切費用，亦即 **Free On Board** 之略語。因此FOB price＝〔製造成本＋國內內陸運費＋包裝費＋裝船雜費＋利潤〕，裝船以後的運費、保險費由買方負擔。FOB多用於進口。理由是進口商支付的外幣只限於出口港的FOB price，之後的運費、保險費則全部以本國貨幣支付，是節約外滙的一種辦法。

3. **CF** 從 CIF 中扣掉保險費（I），即 *CF = FOB + F* 其餘皆與 CIF 同。

4. **FAS** Free Alongside Ship（出口港船邊交貨價），較 FOB 少一項手續費，只負擔在船邊交貨以前的各種費用，即 *FAS = FOB—* LOADING CHARGE。和 FOB 一樣，風險負擔及所有權都在船邊交貨時完全轉移到買方。裝運費、到進口港之前的運費、保險費全部由買方負擔。

5. **EX- SHIP** 是 CIF 的延續，即 *CIF + UNLOADING CHARGE*。進口港洋面船邊交貨價。到進口港將貨卸入買方舢板之前的一切運費、保費、及風險負擔都歸賣方，所有權在裝運文件交予買方前屬於賣方。其他如**碼頭交貨**（**EX- QUAY**）和**保稅倉庫交貨**（**IN BOND**）都是 EX- SHIP 的延伸。

6. **on the look-out for** ～ 需求～

7. **open account with** ～ = enter into relations with ～ 和～開啓商務關係

8. **respectability** = creditability = credit status 信用程度

9. **the mode of doing business** 交易方式

10. **business integrity** 商業的誠實

11. **financial standing** 財務狀況

12. **financial resources** 財力；資力

13. **well-established and reliable firm** 有口皆碑又可靠的公司

14. **credit enquiry** 信用查詢

15. **quotation** 報價；報價單；時價

16. **quote** = state the price of ～

  - to quote one（人）**on**（for）（物品） 報給（人）～物的價格
  - to quote **for**（on）（物品） 報（物品）的價格
  - to quote one's best possible CIF Keelung price
    報到基隆運費、保險費在內的可能最低價
  - to quote us your best possible CIF Keelung price
    報給本公司貴方到基隆運費、保險費在內的可能最低價

17. **as per ～**　按照～。這種用法雖然受到種種批評，但現在商用英文中廣爲使用，可照樣使用無礙。*as per enclosed copy*（ 按照附寄影本 ）。

18. **bankers**　交易銀行
    Please refer us to our bankers, Bank of Taiwan, Taipei.
    請向本公司的交易銀行－台北的台灣銀行查詢。

19. Messrs. 公啓。是 Mr. 的複數，採自法文 Messieurs 簡化而成。用於含有個人名字的機構名稱。
    (1) 擁有 2 名以上男子名稱的公司機構
      Messrs. AB & C = ABC　AB & C 公司公啓
    (2) 含有個人名字的公司組織
      Messrs. Dawson & Co.　　道生公司公啓
      Messrs. Dawson & Sons　道生父子公司公啓
      Messrs. Dawson & Bros.　道生兄弟公司公啓

  ** 不用於一般公司或公家機關名稱上。
    The National Tax Bureau of the Republic of China
    中華民國國稅局公啓

商務・信用查詢模範書信

A. 商務查詢 (Business Enquiry)

1

We have seen your advertisement in " The Metal Worker " and are interested in aluminium screws and fittings of all kinds. Please quote us for the supply of the items listed on *the enclosed enquiry form*, giving your prices CIF Durban. Will you please also state your earliest delivery date, your terms of payment, and discounts for regular purchases? As our *annual requirements in* metal fittings of all kinds are considerable, perhaps you would also send us your catalog and details of your specifications.

本公司在「金屬工作者」上看到貴方的廣告，對各種的鋁螺絲釘和附件深感興趣。請將列在附寄的詢問表中各項目的供應價格，報給我方貴公司到德爾班的運費、保險費在內價。也請貴方說明最早的交貨日期、付款條件、及定期購買的折扣。因為本公司對各種金屬附件每年的需求相當大，或許貴方也願意寄目錄和詳細的說明書給本公司。

➡ aluminium〔ə'lumɪnɪəm〕*n.*〔化〕鋁（金屬元素）
　 fitting〔'fɪtɪŋ〕*n.*(*pl.*) 附件；傢俱

2

Greetings : we have seen your new product OLIVETTI *Portable* Typewriter Model MS-25 at the Taipei Trade Fair. Will you kindly send the catalog thereof, together with the information about the price *on CIF Keelung basis* and other terms involved ?

Looking forward to your early reply,

敬啓者：我方在台北商展上，看到貴公司的新產品奧立維帝 MS-25 型的手提打字機。因此能請貴公司寄來目錄，和以基隆的運費、保險費在內價爲基礎的資料，及其他相關的條件嗎？

期待貴公司早日回覆。

➡ portable〔'portəbl〕*adj.* 可手提的；可移動的
   involved〔ɪn'vɑlvd〕*adj.* 相關的；牽涉在內的

B. 信用查詢（Credit Enquiry）

1

We shall be much obliged if you will kindly give us any confidential information respecting the reputation, *the mode of doing business* and financial standing of Messrs. A & Co., with which we are now planning to *enter into business relations*. Looking forward to having the pleasure of your early reply.

如蒙貴方親切給予本公司，任何有關Ａ公司的商譽、交易方式和財務狀況的機密資料，本公司將非常感激，本公司現在正計劃和Ａ公司締結商務關係。期待貴方早日回信。

➡ confidential〔ˌkɑnfəˈdɛnʃəl〕*adj*. 機密的；參與機密的

2

This is in reply to your enquiry dated April 3 about the credit status of Messrs. A & Co. *As requested*, we immediately contacted various concerns related to the *inquiree firm* to find that it is now being pressed by several creditors and its position is *precarious*. As this is the case, we deem it rather advisable for you to refrain from having relations with that company.

This information is strictly confidential and is given without responsibility on our part.

這是答覆貴方4月3日查詢有關Ａ公司的信用狀況。如貴方所要求的，本公司立刻和與受查詢的公司有關的各種公司連絡，結果發現該公司現在正受一些債權人催迫，而且狀況很危險。既然情況如此，本公司認為，貴方避免和該公司建立關係是相當明智的。這份資料純屬機密，本公司概不負責。

➡ precarious〔prɪˈkɛrɪəs〕*adj*. 危險的；不穩固的

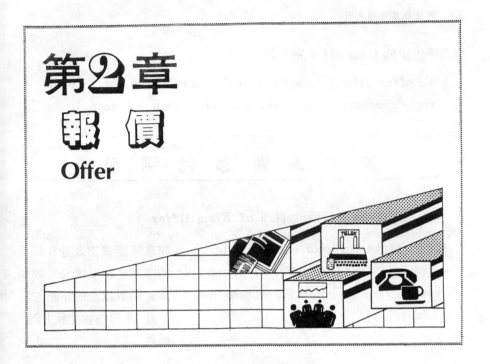

第2章 報價 Offer

1. 確定報價　Firm Offer

　　報價（offer）的定義是報價人向被報價人提出一定的交易條件，通常都是賣方（seller）向買方（buyer）提出的。若是由買方向賣方提出時稱爲 **bid**（出價）。一般報價有**確定報價**（firm offer）、**未定期限報價**（free offer）、**還價**（counter-offer）、**確認後有效的報價**（offer subject to confirmation）、**有權先售報價**（offer subject to prior sale）等等。本單元就從確定報價開始說明，這是賣方對買方開發一定期限內的報價（24小時、48小時、3天、5天、…）在此期限內市價的變動不影響此固定價格，若買方接受，立刻就告成交。可以普通電報或交換電報通知賣方 acceptance，不需正式的確認書。

賣方所提出的 firm offer 形式如下：

> We offer firm 〔 product 〕 at 〔 price 〕, subject to your
> reply reaching us by (*or*, not later than)〔 date 〕.

確 定 報 價 必 備 例 句

A. 提出確定報價(Presentation of Firm Offer)

1. Many thanks for your cable enquiry of March 5, and we *offer firm* subject to your acceptance reaching us by March 11.

非常感謝貴方3月5日的電報查詢，本公司的確定報價以您的承諾在3月11日前寄達我方爲條件。

2. Thank you for your enquiry of April 10, and in reply we *offer firm*, subject to immediate acceptance by cable, OLIVETTI PORTABLE TYPEWRITER MODEL MS−25 at US$144 per unit, CIF BOMBAY.

感謝貴方4月10日的查詢，本公司答覆確定報價，奧立維帝MS−25型手提打字機，到孟買的運費、保險費在內價每台美金144元，但須以立刻用電報承諾爲條件。

3. We *offer firm for acceptance in our hands* by June 20 〔 name of goods 〕 at 〔 price 〕.

本公司〔物品名稱〕〔價格〕的確定報價，須以貴方的承諾在6月20日以前送達我方爲條件。

4. We thank you for your cable en-quiry of March 10 and have just cabled you in reply the following firm offer, **subject to** your ac-ceptance reaching here by March 20.

感謝貴方3月10日的電報查詢，本公司剛打電報給您，答覆下列的確定報價，以3月20日前接到貴方承諾爲條件。

5. We would state that **this offer is firm for three days** and that there is very little likelihood of the goods remaining unsold once this particular offer **has lapsed**.

   ➡ lapse〔læps〕 *v.* 失效

本報價是以三天爲限的確定報價，一旦這項特別報價失效，這些貨品不太可能仍未賣出，特此奉告。

6. This offer must be withdrawn if not accepted within seven days.

如果七天之內未接到承諾，本報價必須撤銷。

提出確定報價的結尾祝福語

1. Awaiting good news,

敬待好消息。

2. We recommend you to **take prompt advantage** of this offer, which is firm for three days only. **With compliments.**

本公司建議貴方迅速利用這項確定報價，因爲只有三天的期限。祝商安。

3. We look forward to your favorable reply.

   ➡ favorable〔ˈfevərəbḷ〕 *adj.* 接受的；贊成的

期待貴方接受的回覆。

4. We look forward to your early order.

期待貴方早日訂貨。

5. We are sure you will *see in this offer a real opportunity*.

本公司確定貴方一定會視這項報價爲絕佳的好機會。

6. We appreciate your *past custom*, and look forward to serving you again now *at the new prices*.

感謝貴方過去的惠顧，期待現在以新價格再爲您效勞。

7. We look forward to the opportunity of *being of service to you*.

期待有爲貴方效勞的機會。

8. We are *at your service* at all times.

本公司隨時待命效勞。

9. We hope you will find our terms and delivery dates acceptable, and we can assure you that you may *count on* our full cooperation in the matter.

希望貴方認爲本公司的條件和交貨日期可以接受，有關此事，我方可向您保證，將鼎力合作。

➡ *count on* 指望；依賴

B. 接受確定報價（ Acceptance of Firm Offer ）

1. We thank you for your *quotation* of March 10 for 〔item〕and are pleased to accept your offer.

感謝貴方3月10日〔項目名稱〕的報價，本公司很樂於接受您的報價。

2. Thank you for your *offer* of March 10, which we accept *on the terms quoted*.

感謝貴方3月10日的報價，在提出的條件下，本公司願意接受。

3. Your quotation of March 10 for 〔item〕has been received and we have pleasure in enclosing our order....

貴方3月10日〔 項目名稱〕的報價已收到，本公司樂於附上訂單…。

4. Many thanks for your *cable offer* of March 10. Your quotation seems *reasonable*, and we deem it possible to *secure* some orders from you.

➡ secure〔sɪ'kjʊr〕*v*. 得到

非常感謝貴方3月10日的電報報價。您的報價似乎很合理，我們有可能向貴公司訂購一些貨品。

5. Thank you very much for your cable offer of March 10, which we think moderate under the present market conditions, and we wish to *place trial orders with you for* 〔item〕.

非常謝謝貴方3月10日的電報報價，我方認爲在目前的市場情況下，價格適中，希望試訂貴方的〔 項目名稱〕。

接受確定報價的結尾語

1. Please confirm our order immediately.

   請立刻確認本公司的訂
   單。

2. Please despatch as quickly as
   possible.

   請儘快寄來。

3. To ensure our order, we are
   ready to open an *L/C* and you
   will be advised of its number upon its establishment. We should be
   grateful if you would arrange for
   shipment *at an early date*.

   為了確保本公司的訂單,
   我方準備開信用狀,一
   開出來就會告知貴方信
   用狀的號碼。若貴方能
   早日安排裝船,則感幸
   甚。

   ➡ L/C = *letter of credit* 信用狀

4. Your prompt *execution* will be
   appreciated.

   貴方儘早履行將不勝感
   激。

5. Kindly advise us when the goods
   will be *despatched*.

   請告知何時出貨。

6. Your early attention to this
   order will be appreciated.

   若蒙貴方早日處理這份
   訂單,則感幸甚。

2.未限定期限報價

　　未限定期限報價（ free offer ）是賣方向買方提出一定的條件，但未限定明確期限。雖然未明示期限，但也絕非一年半載都還有效，一般都是以within a reasonable time（在合理時間內）作為條件。確定後有效報價都是在 free offer 上加條件，即買方承諾後仍需再確認。也就是市場變動（ market fluctuation ）激烈時，可以變更價格或支付條件。即俗稱的**SUBCON**（ **subject to** 〔**final**〕 **confirmation**之略），意思是還需要買賣當事人以書面再確認，不能單靠 cable（ 電報 ）、telex（ 電傳 ）訂定正式契約。SUBCON的英文寫法如下：

　　We offer（quote）, subject to our 〔final〕 confirmation,
　　〔product〕 at 〔price〕....

未 限 定 期 限 報 價 必 備 例 句

A. 提出未限定期限報價（ **Presentation of Free Offer** ）

1. Thank you for your enquiry of
   March 10, and we can quote *you*
   on 〔product〕 *at* 〔price〕....

   感謝貴方3月10日的查詢，本公司對〔產品〕的報價是〔價格〕…。

2. We appreciate your letter of
   March 10 asking for an *offer*
   on 〔product〕, and are pleased
   to quote as follows:

   感謝貴方3月10日來信詢問〔產品〕的報價，本公司樂於報價如下：

3. We trust that you will *see your way to* taking advantage of our fer, and look forward to your early reply.

相信貴方會設法利用本公司的報價，並期待您早日回信。

　➡ *see one's way to* 設法

4. We trust you will be able to accept our offer, which will be *kept open against* your reply by telex.

相信貴方可以接受本公司的報價，此價格需以電傳回覆，方為有效。

5. These goods being in great demand, we *cannot hold this offer open.*

這些貨品需求量很大，本公司無法保持此報價有效。

6. This offer will be *valid only for your reply by telex* without undue delay.

只有在貴方立刻以電傳回覆，本報價才有效。

7. This offer will *remain open* until the receipt of your cable reply.

本報價在收到貴方電報回覆前持續有效。

　➡ *remain open* 持續有效

8. We offer, *subject to our confirmation*, 20 OLIVETTI PORTABLE TYPEWRITERS, MODEL MS—25, at US$140 per unit, CIF SINGAPORE for September shipment.

以本公司的確認為條件，我方提供20台MS—25型的奧立維帝手提打字機，船期9月到新加坡的運費、保險費在內價，每台美金140元的報價。

9. We are pleased to *quote*, subject to our confirmation, *for*（on）20 OLIVETTI PORTABLE TYPE-WRITERS，MODEL MS—25，at US＄140 per unit，CIF SINGAPORE for September shipment.

以本公司的確認爲條件，我方提供20台MS—25型的奧立維帝手提打字機，船期9月到新加坡的運費、保險費在內價，每台美金140元的報價。

10. We think you will *do better* to accept this offer now than by delay be perhaps compelled to agree to others less advantageous.

本公司認爲貴方將明智地現在就接受這項報價，以冤因遲延而或許受迫同意其他較不利的條件。

11. As this special offer is to expire at the end of this month, we shall not be able to *execute your orders* at this price after that.

因爲這項特別的報價這個月底期滿，本公司以後無法以這個價格履行貴方的訂單。

12. These goods being subject to *sharp fluctuations of price*, we cannot *keep the offer open against* your reply by telex.

這些貨品的價格變動往往很大，因此除非貴方以電傳答覆，本公司必須撤回這項報價。

➡ fluctuation〔ˌflʌktʃʊˈeʃən〕*n*. 變動；升降

13. We can offer your Cocoa, Chocolate and other confectionery *on sale or return* at very advantageous terms.

本公司以剩貨可以退還的有利條件，提供貴方可可、巧克力和其他糖果的報價。

14. We could *shade* our prices some - what, but we could in no way *go down to anywhere near the figures* as quoted in your letter.

本公司可以略爲降低價格，但是絕對無法降到接近貴方信中所提的數字。

B. 接受未限定期限報價（Acceptance of Free Offer）

1. Thank you for your offer of March 10, and we shall not hesitate to make use of the same *at the first opportunity*.

謝謝貴方3月10日的報價，如果有機會，我們極樂意利用同樣的報價。

2. We feel grateful for your kind offer, of which we will gladly avail ourselves *at the first opportunity*.

感謝貴方善意的報價，若有機會，我方樂於利用此報價。

3. If, at some future time, we should find occasion to *make use of* your offer, we shall be happy to take advantage of the same.

若將來本公司發現有機會利用到貴方的報價，將很樂於利用同樣的報價。

➡ *make use of* 利用
➡ *take advantage of* 利用

4. We thank you for your offer of March 10, which we accept *on the terms quoted*.

感謝貴方3月10日的報價，在提出的條件下，本公司願意接受。

5. Thank you for your cable offer of March 10, which we think inevitable under the present market conditions, and we wish to *place trial orders with you for* [item].

感謝貴方3月10日的電報報價,本公司認爲在目前的市場情況下 , 這個價錢是不可避免的 , 我方希望試訂貴方的〔品目〕。

3.還價　Counter-Offer

還價（ counter-offer ）就是買方對賣方的報價（ 確定或未限定期限報價 ）提出修正的報價。一旦買方提出還價,賣方原先的報價隨即消滅。通常賣方提出的報價,買方不會立即接受,必定會就價格或支付條件、裝船日期表示意見或要求,賣方當然又會對還價提出異議,經過數次報價、還價的往返交涉方才達成契約。

還　價　必　備　例　句

1. Many thanks for your cable offer of March 10. We agree to your price, but should like to know if you are prepared to *grant* us a discount of 5 percent *for* a quantity of 2,000.

非常感謝貴方 3 月 10日的電報報價。本公司同意貴方的價錢 , 但是想知道數量二千個時 , 貴方是否準備給我方百分之五的折扣 。

2. Thank you very much for your offer of April 10. *Upon checking your offer*, we would like to say

非常感謝貴方 4 月 10日的報價。在查對您的報價後 , 本公司認爲貴方

that your price seems a little higher than we had expected.

的價錢似乎比我方預期的要高些。

3. We thank you for your cable offer of April 10. ***With your offer on hand***, we immediately contacted several ***prospective buyers***, but they all state your quotation is around 20 percent higher than....

感謝貴方4月10日的電報報價。您的報價一送達我方,本公司立刻和一些可能的買主接洽,但是他們都指陳貴方的報價比…高出百分之二十左右。

➡ prospective〔prə′spɛktɪv〕*adj.* 可能的;有望的

4. The proposed terms will ***place our business on a no paying basis***, and therefore, may we ask you to ***go down to anywhere near our figure***, taking into consideration the circumstances in which we are placed?

貴方提出的條件將使本公司的生意無利可圖,因此要求貴方考慮我方所處的情況,把價格降到接近我方的數目。

5. With many thanks we have received your quotation of March 10, to which we can generally agree, but what ***special discount*** can you offer for orders over £ 5,000 net?

我方已收到貴方3月10日的報價,非常感激,大體上我方可以同意,但是訂單超過淨五千英鎊時,貴方可以提供多少特別折扣呢?

6. We appreciate your offer of March 10, but we must point out that the proposed quotation will *leave us little or no margin of profit*. Couldn't you grant us a 5 percent cut in your price so that we may send you large orders？

    感謝貴方３月10日的報價，但是本公司必須指出，貴方提出的報價使我方幾乎無利潤可圖。貴方是否能降價百分之五，使我方可大量訂購?

→ margin〔'mɑrdʒɪn〕*n*. 利潤；盈餘

還價的結尾語

1. Your prompt reply will be appreciated.

    若貴方迅速回覆，則感幸甚。

2. Your kindest and best *attention* to this will be appreciated.

    若貴方親切、周延地處理這件事則感幸甚。

3. We await good news.

    敬待貴方的好消息。

4. We look forward to receiving your favorable reply.

    期待收到貴方同意的回函。

5. We should be highly gratified if you would *see your way to coming down to this price level*, taking into due consideration *the position we are placed in*.

    倘若貴方能適當地考慮本公司所處的境況，而設法降到這個價位，則感幸甚。

6. We could send you large（regular）
   orders if you would **see your way**
   to bringing your price down to a
   level comparable with that of
   your competitors in this market.
   May we have good news from you
   soon.

若貴方能設法把價格降
到可以與這個市場的競
爭者相當的程度，本公
司可以大量（定期）訂
購。希望早日接到您的
好消息。

4. 拒絕報價　Refusal of Offer

當賣方提出的報價和我方條件相差甚遠，或是市場不景氣、購買力
不足、價格過於離譜或我方有困難而不得不回絕時，稱爲**拒絕報價（re-**
fusal of offer）。

拒 絕 報 價 必 備 例 句

1. Thank you very much for your
   letter of March 10 **making an**
   offer on your latest product. To
   our regret, however, we cannot
   make use of your kind offer. The
   reason is that....

非常感謝貴方3月10日
來信提供最新產品的報
價。然而，本公司很遺
憾無法利用貴方善意的
報價。原因是…。

2. We have received your offer of
   March 10, but are sorry to tell
   you that....

貴方3月10日的報價已
經收到，但是我方很抱
歉告訴您…。

3. Thank you for your offer of April 15 for your latest product. After carefully considering your offer, however, we have *come to the conclusion* that....

感謝貴方4月15日對最新產品的報價。然而經過仔細考慮，本公司達成的結論是…。

4. Many thanks for your offer of June 10 for your *latest product* ... We deeply regret, however, to inform you that....

非常感謝貴方6月10日對最新產品…的報價。然而，本公司深感遺憾通知您…。

5. We deeply appreciate your kind offer of March 1 for your *latest product*, but are sorry to have to inform you that....

深深感激貴方3月1日對最新產品善意的報價，但是本公司感到很抱歉必須通知您…。

6. Thank you very much for your offer dated April 18 for your latest product, but it is to our deep regret that we *cannot make use of your kind offer at present*.

非常感謝貴方4月18日對最新產品的報價，但是本公司深感抱歉，目前無法利用貴方善意的報價。

7. Thank you for your quotation for the supply of [item], but we have been obliged to place our order elsewhere *in this instance*.

感謝貴方對供應〔品目〕的報價，但是在這種情況下，本公司不得不向別處訂購。

➡ *in this instance* 在這種情況下

8. We appreciate your offer of a reduced price, but are of the opinion that the market would not
stand an article of this quality
at all.

感謝貴方提供降低的價
格，但是我們認爲本地
的市場將無法接受這種
品質的商品。

9. In consequence of the **slack de-**
mand, we have decided to **drop**
this article, and are very sorry
not to be able to make use of
your kind offer.

由於滯銷，本公司已經
決定放棄這件商品，很
抱歉不能利用貴方善意
的報價。

➡ slack〔slæk〕*adj.* 低迷的；蕭條的

10. Your terms differ so widely from
those offered by our friends that
it is quite impossible for us to
take your offer **into considera-**
tion.

貴方的條件和我方的朋
友提供的條件相差太大，
本公司不可能考慮貴方
的報價。

11. We have **gone very carefully into**
your letter of July 1 advising us
of your quotation (offer), and
regret to say that we cannot **see**
our way to accepting the terms
you offer.

本公司已經愼重研究過
貴方 7 月 1 日來信告知
的報價，很遺憾我方無
法接受貴方所提的條件。

➡ **go into** 研究；調查

12. Under such circumstances, we
    have no choice but to decline your
    kind offer....

在這種情況下，本公司
不得不拒絕貴方善意的
報價… 。

拒絕報價的結尾語

1. *Regretting our inability to meet*
   your kind offer, but soliciting
   your continued favors and attention ,

   ➡ solicit〔səˈlɪsɪt〕*v.* 懇求

很遺憾不能接受貴方善
意的報價，但是懇請貴
方繼續支持和關照 。

2. We hope you will understand the
   circumstances which *compel* us
   to decline your offer.

希望貴方了解迫使本公
司拒絕貴方報價的情況。

3. We are really sorry not *to be*
   helpful, but hope that you will
   understand our position.

本公司不能給予幫助深
感抱歉，但是希望貴方
能了解我方的處境 。

4. We wish you to understand our
   position of *having to* decline your
   offer.

   ➡ decline〔dɪˈklaɪn〕*v.* 拒絕；婉謝

希望貴方能了解本公司
必須拒絕貴方報價的處
境 。

5. *Please accept our apologies for*
   not being helpful to you.

因為不能對貴方有所幫
助，請接受本公司的道
歉 。

6. Under such circumstances, we feel we must return your kind offer, *with our apologies and sincere thanks*.

在這種情況下，本公司覺得必須以歉意和誠摯的感謝回覆貴方善意的報價。

7. Thanking you again for your kindness and looking forward to *your continued favors and attention*,

再次感謝貴方的善意，並期待貴方繼續的支持與關照。

5.有權先售報價　Offer Subject to Prior Sale

這是一種 sales letter 的 circular（通函），即將同一產品的報價同時向多數客戶提出，**先到先售**〔**on a first-come-first-served principle（basis）**〕的報價，其英文寫法如下：

① We offer, subject to prior sale,....

② We offer, subject to the goods being unsold,....

有 權 先 售 報 價 必 備 例 句

1. *We offer, **subject to prior sale**, our latest product at ～〔price〕.*

　　以先到先售爲條件，本公司以～〔價格〕提供最新產品的報價。

➡ *subject to ～* 以～爲條件

2. This time we have developed the newest type of car PEGASUS, streamlined, mobile, less expensive. For details, please refer to the attached catalog and price list. We **hold this offer good only for acceptance** by next Monday, and after that, *it is subject to the goods being unsold*.

　　這次本公司開發流線型、富於機動力、價格便宜的最新型飛馬汽車。詳情請查閱所附的目錄和價目表。只有在下週一前承諾本價爲有效，過期後則以貨物未售出爲條件。

➡ mobile〔＇mobɪl〕*adj*. 富於機動力的

3. The product is now *finding a ready market* and we cannot hold the offer open: we are therefore in a position *to make the offer subject to the goods being unsold* (in stock) on receipt of your order.

本產品正找尋現成的市場，我方不可能維持本報價有效：因此，本公司以在接到貴方訂單時貨物未售出（有存貨）為條件報價。

4. The prices quoted are subject to the *goods being in stock on* receipt of orders.

所報的價格以接到訂單時尚有存貨為條件。

有權先售報價的結尾語

1. Awaiting your early orders,

敬待貴方早日訂貨。

2. Looking forward to the pleasure of having your early order,

期待有幸早日接到貴方的訂單。

3. We are sure that you will *find in this offer a real opportunity*.

相信貴方一定會發現本報價實在是個好機會。

4. We expect that a rush of orders will *come in* soon and we fear that a delay in placing orders would miss the excellent chance of securing the goods in your hands. We look forward to your earliest orders.

預期大量訂單不久就到來，本公司惟恐遲延下訂單貴方將失去貨物到手的絕佳良機。期待貴方早日下訂單。

6.出價 Bid

買方向賣方要求的購入報價稱爲 bid。有期限的出價稱爲 **firm bid**（**遞實價**），與賣方向買方提出的 firm offer（確定報價）是相對的。買方所提出的價格稱爲「**限價**」（ limit ），此外，當國內買方委託國外的第三者代購物品，提呈給受託購買者的買方價格也稱爲限價。這時**委託購買者**叫 indentor ，**受託購買者**稱爲 indentee 。（參考第四章「訂單」）

出 價 必 備 例 句

A. 向賣方提出出價（ Presentation of Bid to Seller ）

1. Will you *be good enough to telex us* if you can accept our order *at our limit* ?

   能否請貴公司以電傳通知，您是否願以我方的限價接受訂單？

2. We *bid firm* US$700 per unit *for* your latest product, COMPUTERIZED SEWING MACHINE MODEL MC—25. Please telex us by next Monday if you can accept our bid.

   貴方的新產品MC—25型電腦縫紉機，本公司遞實價爲每台美金七百元。若貴方能接受我方的出價，請在下週一前以電傳通知我方。

3. We authorize you to make the shipment at any time before next spring, provided you can *buy at our limit*.

假使貴方能以本公司的限價買進,我方可授權給貴方在明年春天之前隨時裝運。

4. If *our limits* are unworkable, please telex the additional percentage you *require on the prices*.

如果本公司的限價不可行,請以電傳通知貴方在本價格上要求附加的比率。

5. We are planning to *place regular orders with* you for the goods listed below, and could you admit our limits as specified on the table? Looking forward to your favorable reply,

我方正計畫定期訂購下列貨品,貴方能答應我方在這張表中指明的限價嗎?敬待貴方同意的回函。

【 說明 】 委託購買人和受託購買人之間的往來函件,請參閱第四章「訂單」。

B. 賣方回覆買方的出價 (Seller's Reply to Bid)

1. Your bid of March 24 has *received our attention*. After carefully checking the same, we regret to say that your limits fall pretty below our prices *leaving no margin of profit*.

貴方3月24日的出價已知悉。經仔細查對的結果,貴方的限價低於我方的價錢太多,使我方無利潤可圖,深以爲憾。

2. Your order cannot be executed
   not only on account of prices a-
   bove your limits ***but*** the freight
   also.

貴方的訂單不能被履行，
不只因為價錢超過貴方
的限價，也因為運費的
關係。

3. It is impossible for us to execute your order ***at the price***
   stipulated, in consequence of the
   quantity of your order being too
   small.

由於貴方的訂單數量太
小，以貴方堅持的價格，
本公司不可能履行您的
訂單。

C. 受託購買者回覆委託購買者 (Indentee's Reply to Indentor)

1. We fear your limits are unworkable; we are, however, making
   enquiries ***all around the market***.

恐怕貴方的限價不可行;
然而，本公司正在市場
上到處查詢。

2. We are afraid that the prices
   have ***run*** slightly higher than your
   limits, but we would look round
   in the market so as to secure
   you at the prices named.

恐怕價格比貴方的限價
稍微高些，但是本公司
會在市場上仔細調查，
以確保貴方開出的價格。

3. In view of the long continuance of
   your patronage, we shall do our utmost to do at the limit despite ***the***
   enhanced cost of production.

鑒於貴方長期持續的惠
顧，雖然生產成本提高，
本公司仍將盡力以限價
成交。

➡ patronage〔'petrənɪdʒ〕 *n*. 惠顧

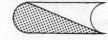 報　價　須　知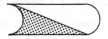

1. 往來文件中貨品的名稱極其重要，爲了引起對方注意，最好將所有貨品名稱或第一個字母大寫。

2. 對於詢問函的回覆，首先應表示感謝，再告知對方價格條件，最後以「期待回信」「期待訂購」作結。

3. 詢問目標可從目錄、價目表、資料到具體的「極欲購買，請告知付款條件及其他」，所以回覆亦應斟酌採未限定期限報價，到確定報價的其中一項。

4. 貿易上的期限都是採取到達我方的日期爲標準。

　　電報　offering until May 10 here

　　　　　offering firm May 10 here

　　信函　subject to your reply reaching here (us) by (not later than) May 10

5. 「對～以〔價格〕報價」

　　a）make an offer **on** (**for**) 〔item〕 **at** 〔price〕

　　b）offer 〔item〕 at 〔price〕

6. 「折扣報價」

　　a）to make an offer of a reduced price

　　b）to make an offer of ～ percent discount

　　c）an offer to make a discount of ～ percent

7. 「對～的報價」

　　quotations **for** (**on**) ～

8. 「對～品目報價～」
   we **quote** you **on**（**for**）〔item〕at〔price〕

9. 「為～的降低價格」　be underquoted **by**～

10. 「開出較公定價低的價格」　underquote official rates

11. 「開出比競爭對手便宜 5 ％的價格」
    to underquote the competitors by 5 percent
    Some merchants underquote makers to the extent of one
    to three dollars per ton.
    有些商人開出每噸較廠商便宜一到三元的價格。

12. **order 的用法**
    a)　to **place** orders **for**（貨品）**with**（對象）
    b)　to order（貨品）from（對象）
    c)　trial order 試購訂單
    d)　sample order 樣品訂單
    e)　goods on order 訂單上的貨品

13. 「拍發電傳給～」（作動詞用）　to telex（person, place, *etc.*）
    Telex Australia that prices are to be increased 10 per-
    cent.
    電傳通知澳洲，價格將提高百分之十。
    「拍發電傳給～通知～」（作動詞用）　to telex the message
    to ～

14. see *one's* way to ～ 想法做～，設法～ （常用於商用英文的請
    託信函中）

15. to **hold**（**keep**）an offer **open**（**good, valid**）
    保持報價仍然有效

We cannot **keep** the offer **open against** your reply by telex.

若不以電傳回覆，我方將撤回報價。

against = in preparation for 也就是說上面的翻譯源自「我們
不能一直等待電傳回覆而維持原報價」，以下用法亦同。

The offer will be **kept open against** your reply by telex.

本報價需以電傳回覆方爲有效。

The offer will be kept open until Monday morning.

本報價到星期一上午仍然有效。

16. **on sale or return** 以剩貨可退還爲條件

We offer you the following goods **on sale or return** at the
prices advantageous to you.

下列貨品以剩貨可退還的有利條件報價。

17. subject to the goods being unsold（in stock）on receipt of
order

以收到訂單時 貨物未售出爲條件

18. **shade** the price 略微降低價格

19. **go down to** somewhere near the figures quoted

請把價格降低到接近我們提出的數字。

報 價 模 範 書 信

A. 接受報價時 (Acceptance of Offer)

1

Many thanks for your prompt reply of April 20 to our enquiry for BELL-WIRE. We enclose our *official order* for 15,000 yards, which we understand you can supply from stock. As indicated in our first enquiry, the quality must *be up to* the sample we sent you, and the weight and color of the cotton insulation *identical to* that of the sample. Our order is placed on this condition.

非常感謝貴方4月20日即時答覆本公司對電鈴鐵絲的查詢。茲附上一萬五千碼的正式訂單，我方知道此數量貴方可以從存貨供應。如我方首次查詢所指出的，品質必須與我方寄去的樣品一致，而棉絕緣體的重量和顏色必須和樣品完全相同。本訂單是以此條件發出的。

➡ official〔ə'fɪʃəl〕*adj.* 正式的；公務上的
➡ insulation〔,ɪnsə'leʃən〕*n.*〔電〕絕緣體；絕緣材料

2

Thank you for your letter of January 12, with which you sent us details of PLASTIC WARE. We have now seen samples of these goods and are prepared to *give them a trial*, provided you can guarantee delivery on or before March 1. The enclosed order is given strictly on this condition, and we *reserve the right of* cancellation and refusal of delivery after this date.

感謝貴方1月12日來信,並寄來貴方的塑膠製品的詳情,本公司現已看過這些貨物的樣品,若貴方能保證3月1日或在此之前交貨,本公司準備試購。附上的訂單以嚴守此項條件下發出,我方保留超過期限解約和拒絕提貨的權利。

➡ guarantee〔, gærən'ti〕 *v*. 保證;擔保

B. 還價(Counter-offer)

1

We thank you for your quotation of 〔price〕 per yard for Cloth No. 110. Before placing our order, we should like to know whether you can *give us a slightly better price* for this material. *We have in mind* an order for some 2,000 yards, and as the cloth is for export to a highly competitive market, a keen price is essential. Your prompt reply would be appreciated.

感謝貴方第 110 號布每碼〔價格〕的報價。我方在發出訂單前,想知道這種布料貴方是否可以給我方稍低的價格。本公司打算訂購二千碼左右,因為這種布是要外銷到高度競爭的市場,便宜的價格是必要的。若貴方即時答覆,則不勝感激。

➡ essential〔ə'sɛnʃəl〕*adj.* 必要的;重要的

2

We have received both your quotation of February 1 and the samples of MEN'S SUITINGS, and thank you for these. While appreciating the good quality of your suitings, we find the prices of these materials rather *high for the market* we wish to supply. We have also to point out that very good suitings are now available in Eastern countries from several European manufacturers, and all of these are *at prices from 10 to 15* percent below yours. We should like to place our order with you, but must ask you to consider whether you can make a more favorable offer. As our order would be worth around $ 5,000, you may think it *worth while* to make a concession.

我方已收到貴方2月1日的報價和男裝衣料的樣品，非常感謝。在讚賞貴方衣料品質良好時，也發現這些質料的價格對我方想供應的市場來說相當高。同時也必須指出，現在東方國家可以從一些歐洲製造商得到非常好的衣料，而且價格都比貴方的低百分之十到十五。本公司想下訂單給貴方，但必須請貴方考慮是否可以提供更有利的報價。因爲我方的訂單值美金五千元左右，貴方或許會認爲讓步是值得的。

➡ suiting〔'sjutɪŋ〕*n*. 衣料

➡ concession〔kən'sɛʃən〕*n*. 讓步

C. 拒絕報價（ Refusal of Offer ）

1

Many thanks for your offer, dated November 21, of 1,000 lb. Brazilian Coffee. We regret being unable to make use of this consignment as the price you ask is above *the market level here* for the quality in question. The coffee supplied last year from this *source* was not of the quality we had expected for the price quoted.

非常感謝貴方 11 月 21 日對一千磅巴西咖啡的報價。因為就談到的品質而言，貴方要求的價格高於這裏的市場水平，我方很遺憾不能利用這次的託售。去年這個來源供應的咖啡，品質與提出的價格並不相當。

➡ lb. = librae = pounds 磅

第3章
契　約
Contract; Agreement

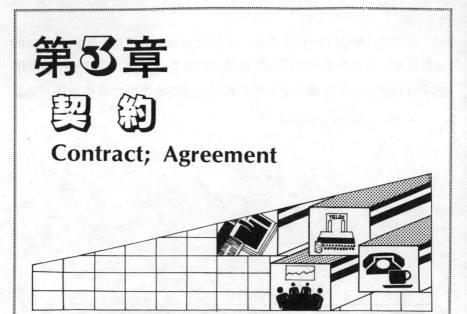

　　賣方向買方提呈報價單，經由買方接受（accept），或多次與賣方交換 counter-offer 之後，才能達到訂定契約的階段。此時①買方需擬定**銷售確認書**（Sales Note），買方也需擬定**購買確認書**（Purchase Note），分別寄送給對方審查。②買方基於賣方所提供的資料做成訂單（order），送交賣方，賣方審查之後，再寄送**訂單確認書**（Confirmation of Order）給買方。如此，訂定契約的手續才算完成。

　　若爲大宗買賣，內容複雜，因此，賣方需擬定**契約**（Contract，Agreement）（正副本兩份）寄送買方，買主審查內容之後，就在正副二份契約上簽名，自己保留正本，將副本寄還賣方。其主要內容有契約號碼，商品明細表、數量、價格、包裝法、保險條件、裝船日期、付款條件。

契　約　必　備　例　句

1. Please note that this *was stipulated by contract*.

請注意本件係由契約所規定。

2. Confirming our exchange of cables, we enclose the *captioned sales note for*....

爲確認雙方電報往返起見，本公司隨函奉寄…的有標題的銷售確認書。

➡ captioned〔'kæpʃənd〕*adj.* 加有標題的；附插圖或照片的

3. We are pleased to confirm having sold to you the following goods on the terms and conditions set forth below.

本公司樂於確認，根據下列約定與條件，已售出以下的商品給貴方。

4. We are sorry to *have to* inform you that we are not prepared to renew your contract.

本公司很抱歉必須通知貴方，我方尚未備妥與您重訂契約。

5. *This breach of condition* on your part in respect of delivery is understood to be the cancellation of the whole contract.

關於交貨方面，貴方違反規定，據了解將導致全部契約作廢。

➡ delivery〔dɪ'lɪvərɪ〕*n.* 交貨
➡ cancellation〔ˌkænsə'leʃən〕*n.* 作廢；取消

6. We thank you for your letter of March 19, ***placing an order*** for our Computer Model-16 and enclose Sales Note for your signature and prompt return.

貴方於3月19日來信,訂購16型電腦,本公司很感謝並隨函奉寄銷售確認書,請在上面簽名,並儘快寄回。

7. In respect of the contract, we ***are***, of course, ***bound to*** deliver the machines ***even at a sacrifice***.

契約方面,我方當然有義務交付這些機械,即使是虧本出售。

8. The enclosed agreement and report will render your solicitor and yourself fully acquainted with the particulars as to prices, terms and time.

隨函奉寄的契約書與報告書將會使您及您的律師充分熟知,像價格,條件及時間這類的細節。

→ solicitor〔 sə'lɪsətə 〕 *n.* 律師

9. If you refer to our contract, you will see that we did not promise delivery earlier than May 5.

如果貴方參照本公司的契約,您將明白我方未曾答應過,在5月5日以前交貨。

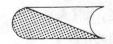 契 約 須 知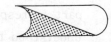

1. **breach of contract** 違反契約

2. **nonfulfillment of contract** 不履行契約

3. **to enter into（conclude）an agreement（a contract）with ～** 與～締結（結束）契約

4. **as per contract** 按照契約

5. **even at a sacrifice** 即使是虧本出售

6. **as arranged** 按照約定 ⎫
 as agreed 按照條件 ⎭ 大體上意思相同

契 約 模 書 信 範

發出銷售確認書（Despatch of Sales Note）

1

Thank you very much for your telex F-E 350 dated June 30 accepting our offer *on condition of* 5 percent cut in the proposed price. After carefully considering your counter-offer, we have agreed to your conditions and immediately drawn up the SALES NOTE, which we airmailed to you today. We hope *you will find it in order* and look forward to your early reply.

　　非常感謝貴方於6月30日拍發的F-E 350商務交換電報，在照提議的價格減少百分之五的條件下，接受本公司的報價。經過審慎考慮您的還價之後，我方已同意您提出的條件，並立刻草擬此買賣契約書，於本日以航空郵件寄上。望您查收，並盼您儘早回覆。

➡ offer〔ˊɔfɚ, ɑfɚ〕*n.* 報價　　counter-offer 還價
　　in order 安然；完好無損地

2

We have accepted your counter-offer by telex of May 10 for 500 dozens of Nylon Stocking S/No. 600 at US＄15 per doz, CIF San Francisco. In confirmation of this order, we enclose Sales Note No. 570. We shall be highly grateful if you will arrange to open an Irrevocable Letter of Credit by cable *in our favor* to enable us to *effect June shipment*, as arranged.

　　本公司已接受貴方於5月10日拍發的電傳還價，以每雙美金15元，到舊金山運費、保費在內價，向我方訂購500雙，S／No. 600 的尼龍長襪。確認此一訂單，我方隨函奉寄570號銷售確認書。倘貴方能安排好以電報開立一張不可撤銷信用狀，以俾於我方六月船運能按照約定，如期完成，我方將不勝感激。

➡ CIF = *cost, insurance & freight* 運費、保費在內價；起岸價
　　Irrevocable Letter of Credit 不可撤消信用狀

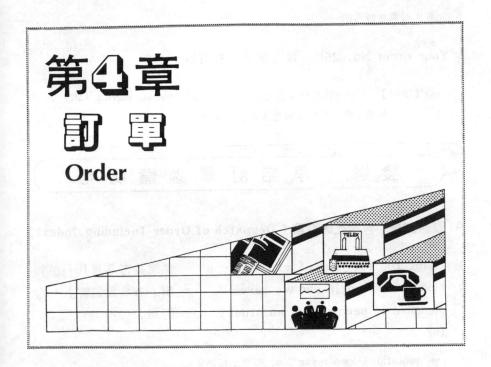

第4章
訂單
Order

1. 發送·承諾訂單　Despatch & Acceptance of Order

　　訂購關係開始於買方詢價，接著是賣方提呈報價單，一直到買方下訂單，才到達貿易的重心階段。訂單可能是買方個人直接簽發給賣方的，也可能是國內廠商簽發給國外第三者全權代理的**代購訂單**（ Indent ），這時**委託訂購人**稱為 indentor ，**受託訂購人**則是 indentee 。

　　若為**確定訂單**（ firm order ），廠商或出口商必須在指定期限內將貨物送交進口商，否則進口商得以拒絕收貨。此外，order 除了「訂單、訂貨、訂購」的意思外，也是票據上所謂的「擡頭人，指定人」，須視前後關係判斷。另外，「訂單」又可說成 order sheet ， order form 。

Your order No. 250＝貴方第 250 號訂單。

【說明】 在發送貨物時，貨品必須印上嘜頭（ *shipping mark* ）（第六章
「裝運」中，「貨櫃輸送須知」第 21 條）。

發 送、承 諾 訂 單 必 備 例 句

A. 發送訂單，包括代購訂單（ Despatch of Order lncluding lndent ）

1. Thank you for your offer (quotation) of March 16 and we have
pleasure in sending you an order
for....

   感謝貴方 3 月 16 日的報
   價，有幸爲您寄上…的
   訂單。

   ➡ quotation〔 kwo'teʃən 〕 *n*. 報價；報價單

2. Many thanks for your quotation
of March 16 for the supply of
your latest production...and we
should like to place a *trial
order*.

   非常感謝貴方 3 月 16 日
   供應最新產品…的報價，
   本公司願意發出試購訂
   單。

3. We have duly received your quotation of March 16 and enclose
our *official order* for....

   本公司已適時收到貴方
   3 月 16 日的報價單，玆
   隨函奉寄我方對…的正
   式訂單。

4. Please supply *the nearest you have
to* the enclosed sample.

   請貴方供應與附寄樣品
   最類似的產品。

5. As we are out of this line, please send *the nearest you have* in stock.

由於本公司已無此種貨品，請寄上貴方存貨中最類似的產品。

6. Thank you very much for your quotations of March 16 and we enclose our *Indent* No. ～ for [goods] and should be glad if you would effect shipment *with all possible speed*.

非帶感謝貴方3月16日的報價，本公司隨函附上對〔貨品〕第～號代購訂單，並盼您儘快完成裝船。

7. Our *Indent* No. ～ is enclosed, and we should be glad if you would arrange....

隨函奉寄本公司第～號代購訂單，若蒙貴方安排…則感幸甚。

8. We have pleasure in sending you an *Indent for* immediate shipment....

有幸為貴方寄上…即期裝運的代購訂單。

9. We have much pleasure in sending you an *Indent in confirmation of* our telex message of March 16.

有幸為貴方寄上代購訂單，以確認我方3月16日的電傳電報。

10. Thank you very much for your letter of September 10 enclosing order No. ～ and today we *placed a firm order with* the manufacturer for shipment from Kaohsiung at the end of October.

非常感謝貴方9月10日附有第～號訂單的來函，本公司於今日發送確定訂單給製造商，以便於10月底在高雄裝船。

11. Thank you for your letter of
March 16, with which you sent us
details of your PLASTIC WARE.
We have now seen samples of
these goods and are prepared to
give them a trial, provided you
can guarantee delivery on or before April 10.

感謝貴方3月16日來函，
並附寄塑膠製品的詳情。
本公司已見過這些產品
的樣品，若您能保證在
4月10日或之前交貨，
我方準備試購。

發送訂單，包括代購訂單的結尾語

1. Your early attention to this order will be appreciated.

如蒙貴方及早處理本訂
單，不勝感激。

2. Please note that delivery is required by 〔date〕.

請注意須於〔日期〕前
交貨。

3. If this first *order* is satisfactorily *executed*, we shall place
another order with you.

倘若這張初次訂單被圓
滿履行，本公司將下給
貴方另一張訂單。

4. Your prompt execution of our order will be appreciated.

如蒙貴方卽時履行本公
司的訂單，不勝感激。

5. Kindly advise us when the goods
will be despatched.

請告知本公司貨品將於
何時發送。

6. Your arrangement for early shipment would be appreciated.

如蒙貴方安排及早裝運，
不勝感激。

7. We are ready to open an L/C upon your acceptance of our order.

一俟貴方承諾本公司訂
單，我方即準備開信用
狀。

8. Your prompt reply will be appreciated.

如蒙即時答覆，不勝感
激。

9. If our terms are acceptable to
   you, we hope for your prompt
   execution.

倘若貴方能夠接受本公
司的條件，我方盼望您
即時履行。

10. We would like to hear from you
    soon *in this instance*.

在此情況下，本公司盼
望貴方能早日回函。

B. 承諾訂單，包括代購訂單（Acceptance of Order Including Indent）

1. Thank you very much for your order of March 19....

非常感謝貴方3月19日
的訂單…。

2. We have received your order of
   March 19....

本公司已收到貴方3月
19日的訂單…。

3. Very many thanks for your letter
   of March 19, enclosing your order *for*....

萬分感謝貴方3月19日
附有…訂單的來函。

4. Many thanks for your letter requesting the *shipment* of....

十分感謝貴方要求裝運
…的來函。

5. Please accept our thanks for your order of March 16.

萬分感激貴方3月16日的訂單。

6. We are very grateful to you for your kind order of March 19....

本公司非常感激貴方3月19日的訂單。

7. Your order is *receiving our immediate attention* and....

本公司正即刻處理貴方的訂單，並…。

8. Please accept our hearty thanks for your order of March 19 for....

對貴方於3月19日…的訂單，本公司不勝感激。

9. *You may rely on us* to *carry out* your *instructions* in every detail.

您可以信賴我方必徹底遵照貴方的指示執行。

10. *Special instructions* have been given to our despatch department to send your orders on 〔date〕. You may be sure that your wishes will be *carried out*.

本公司已特別指示發送部門，於〔日期〕寄出貴方所訂購的貨品。您的意願必可達成。

11. The goods are nearly ready for despatch and we should be glad to have your instructions.

貨品已大致準備妥當，敬待貴方的指示即可發運。

12. As you do not give any special *instructions for* forwarding, we are *passing your order to* our forwarding agent in the usual way.

由於貴方對發運並未給予任何特殊指示，本公司依往例將您的訂貨轉給我方的發運代理。

13. We have the pleasure to *acknowledge* the receipt of your Indent No. ～ dated ～ , for which we are much obliged.

本公司十分榮幸收到貴方於～日的第～號代購訂單，不勝感激。

14. We have received your letter of March 17 *covering* your Indent No. ～ .

貴方 3 月17日附有第～號代購訂單的來函，本公司業已收悉。

15. We are very grateful to you for your Indent No. ～ .

本公司十分感謝貴方第～號代購訂單。

16. Thank you very much for your letter of March 19 instructing us to buy....

承蒙貴方於 3 月19日來函，指示本公司購買…,不勝感激。

17. We have received your instructions of March 19 for the *purchase* of [item]. We regret, however, that owing to the market conditions here, it is difficult to buy *at your limits*.

本公司業已收到貴方 3 月19日對購買〔產品〕的指示。然而，甚感抱歉，由於本地的市場狀況，甚難以您的限價購得。

18. We are very grateful to you for your Indent No. ～ for [items]. *To our regret*, however, we are unable to accept your order at the prices requested (named).

對貴方〔產品〕第～號代購訂單，本公司不勝感激。然而，萬分遺憾，我方無法依您要求（提出）的價格接受訂單。

承諾訂單，包括代購訂單的結尾語

1. Thanking you again for your orders and looking forward to your *continued attention*,

   對貴方的訂單再致謝忱，並盼您繼續關照。

2. We are *always at your service*.

   本公司隨時待命效勞。

3. If the above conditions *are acceptable to* you, we are ready to arrange for immediate shipment.

   若上述條件可爲貴方接受，本公司準備安排即期裝運。

4. Looking forward to the pleasure of having your *increased orders*,

   期盼有幸得到更多訂單。

5. We *assure* you always *of* our best attention.

   本公司隨時等候貴方指教。

6. You *may rely on us* always to give you prompt attention.

   貴方可以相信，我方隨時迅速履行貴方訂單。

7. Immediate shipment is guaranteed *upon receipt of* your credit.

   一旦接獲貴方信用狀，保證即期裝運。

8. We will do *our very best for you* at any time.

   本公司將隨時盡全力爲貴方效勞。

2.拒絕·取消訂單 Refusal or Cancellation of Order

　　當賣方拒絕訂單時，首先須感謝對方所簽發的訂單，然後鄭重說明拒絕的理由，最後再表示希望今後對方仍然能夠給予支持和惠顧。

　　當買方要撤銷已簽發出的訂單時，必須告訴對方原因，是因賣方未履行義務或遲遲未交貨，或是買方有不得已的苦衷，並將可能產生的後果告訴對方。

拒 絕 · 取 消 訂 單 必 備 例 句

A. 拒絕訂單 (Refusal of Order)

1. Thank you very much for your order
of March 10, but to our regret, our
stock is completely *exhausted* (*or*, we
do not stock the sizes required, *or*,
these colors are no longer available).

承蒙貴方3月10日的訂單，不勝感激。然而，萬分遺憾，本公司已無存貨。（或：本公司並無所需尺寸的存貨；這些顏色已售完。）

➡ exhaust〔ɪg'zɔst〕*v.* 用盡

2. With many thanks, we have received your order of March 10.
We are sorry to say, however,
that these items are now *out of*

承蒙貴方3月10日的訂單，不勝感激。然而，至感抱歉，您所需項目已無存貨，本公司可改

stock, and we can offer you instead the nearest...which is *in no way* inferior to your requirement.

提供您最類似的產品…，品質絕不較您要求的遜色。

3. Many thanks for your order of March 10 for 〔item〕, but we have to explain that....

萬分感謝貴方3月10日〔產品〕的訂單，然而，本公司必須解釋…。

4. Thank you very much for the order *specified* in your letter of March 10. After carefully considering it, we have come to the conclusion that....

十分感謝貴方3月10日來函中所列出的訂單。經仔細考慮後，本公司已決定…。

5. Thank you very much for your *fresh order* of March 30, but have to inform you that production difficulties force us *to decline* further orders *for this model* for the time being.

承蒙貴方3月30日的再購訂單，不勝感激。然而必須通知您，由於生產上的困難，迫使我方不得不暫時婉謝再訂購此類型產品。

6. Under such circumstances, we are not able to promise delivery before next spring, and we feel we must return your order *with apologies and best thanks*.

於此情況下，本公司無法答應於明春前交貨。因此我方覺得應退回您的訂單，並再致上歉意與最高謝意。

7. Thank you for your order of
   March 10 for.... We regret,
   however, to tell you that we are
   at present supplying *only to
   wholesalers*, and therefore, *refer
   you to* Messrs. ～ , who would be
   pleased to meet your needs.

十分感謝貴方3月10日
…的訂單。然而,至感
抱歉,本公司目前只供
應批發商,因而建議您
與～公司接洽,對方必
萬分樂意滿足您的需要。

8. Many thanks for your order of
   March 10 for [item]. We regret,
   however, to tell you that at
   present there is *no demand* here
   for material of the type you submit as a sample, and that we
   shall not manufacture further
   supplies of this line.

承蒙貴方3月10日對
〔產品〕的訂單,不勝
感激。然而,本公司感
到十分抱歉,目前本地
對於您所提樣品的型式,
並無需求。我方也將不
再繼續生產此型貨品。

9. *Much as* we should like to do
   business with you, we fear we
   cannot turn out the carpet of
   reasonable quality at the price
   you ask.

雖然本公司亟望與貴方
有交易往來,然而我方
恐怕依您要求的價格,
製不出相當品質的地毯。

   ➡ *turn out* 製造;生產

10. Supplies of raw materials are
    getting difficult to obtain and we
    have *no alternative but to* decline
    your order.

原料的供應日趨困難,
因而本公司不得不婉謝
貴方的訂單。

11. With many thanks we have received your order of March 10, and are sorry to tell you that we have *a waiting list of* several hundred for these goods and can give no guarantee of delivery this year.

接獲貴方3月10日的訂單，不勝感激。然而，至感抱歉，這些貨品有數百位等待者，因而無法保證於今年交貨。

12. Very many thanks for your kind order of March 10, but we are sorry to say that our factory is at present *fully occupied with* contract orders, and we are obliged to decline your order.

萬分感謝貴方3月10日的訂單。令本公司感到十分抱歉的是，我方工廠目前已全被合約訂單所佔滿，因而不得不婉謝您的訂單。

➡ *be occupied with* ～ 被～佔滿

13. We regret to inform you that an unforeseen scarcity of raw materials renders us unable to execute your order No. ～ by〔date〕, *as arranged.*

本公司十分遺憾地通知貴方，由於未預料到的原料短缺，我方無法依計畫在〔日期〕前履行您第～號訂單。

14. It is with great regret that we find ourselves compelled to ask for *an extension of time in the execution of your order* No. ～ of〔date〕.

至感抱歉，對於貴方〔日期〕第～號訂單，本公司不得不請求延期履行。

➡ *feel compelled to* 不得不

拒絕訂單（包括代購訂單）的結尾語

1. Regretting our inability to **meet
   your requirements**, but looking
   forward to your continued orders,

   對於本公司無法答應貴
   方的要求，至感抱歉，
   但亟盼您能繼續惠予訂
   單。

2. As this is the case, we are very
   sorry that we have to return
   your order **with our apologies
   and best thanks**. Looking forward
   to your continued favors and attention.

   由於此種情況，本公司
   十分遺憾必須退回貴方
   的訂單，並致上我方的
   歉意與最高謝意。同時
   亟盼您繼續關愛惠顧。

3. We are really sorry not to be
   helpful, but hope that you will
   understand our position.

   不能有所助益，本公司
   至感抱歉。但盼貴方能
   了解我方立場。

4. We hope you will **understand** the
   circumstances which compel us to
   decline your order.

   甚盼貴方能了解迫使本
   公司婉謝貴方訂單的情
   況。

5. Our difficulties are only **tempo-
   rary** and we shall welcome your
   orders in the future.

   本公司的困難只是暫時
   的，歡迎貴方將來繼續
   訂購。

6. Of course, we will advise you **as
   soon as** we are able to supply
   these goods again.

   當然，本公司能再度供
   應這些貨品時，必會立
   即通知貴方。

7. Though we failed to meet your requirements *in this instance*, yet we are ready to serve you at any time *if it is within our power*.

雖然本公司於此事無法答應貴方的要求，不過只要在我方能力範圍內，必隨時準備為您提供服務。

8. *Do let us* have other enquiries at any time, as we shall be *only too pleased* to meet them if it is within our power.

務祈隨時向本公司查詢其他價格，因為只要在能力範圍內，我方很樂意接受。

9. We look forward to your prompt reply.

期待貴方即時回覆。

10. We shall be very much grateful if you will agree to our wish, *taking into due consideration* the circumstances we are placed in.

若貴方能適度考慮本公司所處狀況，並同意我方要求，則感幸甚。

B. 取消訂單（ Cancellation of Order ）

1. Your shipment of our order No. ~ has not yet reached us *to date*, notwithstanding our repeated requests for early delivery, and we are obliged to cancel this order.

雖然本公司一再請求及早送貨，但貴方對我方第～號訂單的船運至今尚未到達，因而我方不得不取消此訂單。

➡ notwithstanding〔'nɑtwɪθ'stændɪŋ〕*prep.* 雖然

2. We have already written to you
   twice *urging* despatch of our order No. ～ , but you have failed
   even to give a reply to date, and
   we are compelled to cancel this
   order.

本公司已兩度去函，促
請發送我方第～號訂單
的貨品，但您甚至至今
沒有任何回覆，我方不
得不取消此訂單。

3. Your shipment of our order No.
   ～ *is not yet to* reach us to date.
   Unless it is delivered by the end
   of this month, we have no alter-
   natives but *respectfully* to cancel
   this order.

貴方對本公司第～號訂
單的船運至今尚未到達。
除非在本月底前能夠送
達，我方只得取消此訂
單。

4. We have not yet received our order No. ～ *to this date*. They are
   season goods and late delivery
   will deal us a heavy blow. The
   failure of their arrival by the end
   of this month will force us to
   cancel all *standing orders*.

本公司至今尚未收到第
～號訂單的貨品。彼等
均爲季節性貨品，延遲
交貨會使我方遭受重大
損失。若在本月底前仍
無法送達，我方將不得
不取消目前的一切訂單。

取消訂單的結尾語

1. For all consequences arising
   therefrom（from cancellation），
   we consider that you *are all held*
   liable.

本公司認爲貴方對從此
（取消）而引起之一切
後果，均應負全責。

2. We await your immediate reply.

恭候貴方即時回覆。

3. As this is the case, there is no alternative for us but to cancel our order, *which you will please note*.

有鑑於此，本公司不得不取消訂單，敬請查照。

C. 對取消訂單的回信（ Reply to Cancellation of Order ）

1. We have received your letter proposing to cancel all your orders. The matter was *a great shock to* us because....

本公司已收到貴方取消所有訂單的來函。我方對此事至感震驚，因⋯。

2. We very much regret that you have decided upon cancellation of your order *owing to*....

貴方因⋯而決定取消訂單，本公司至感遺憾。

取消訂單回信的結尾語

1. Regretting our inability to meet your requirements through our *failure in*..., but looking forward to your continued favors and attention,

由於我方未能⋯，以致無法符合貴方需求，至感遺憾。但亟盼您今後繼續關愛惠顧。

2. We feel much regret to have been unable to meet your wishes through *some hitch* on our

由於我方在履行貴方第～號訂單時發生阻礙，致使無法達成您的需求，

part in the execution of your Order No. ～ and express our deep-
est apologies for the *mishap*. We
will *do all in our power* not to
repeat such a failure in future
and look forward to your continued favors and attention.

至感遺憾，並對此一不
幸的發生致上最深歉意。
我方將盡一切努力避免
今後再犯此失誤，並亟
盼您繼續關愛惠顧。

➡ hitch〔hɪtʃ〕*n.* 阻礙

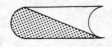 訂　　單　　須　　知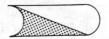

1. **in this〔particular〕instance** 在此情況下

2. **at** *one's* **limits** 以～的限價　**limits = limit prices** （複數）
   limit = limit price （單數）

3. **repeat order, fresh order** 再購訂單
   rush order 緊急訂單
   to renew order 再次訂購

4. **a waiting list of one hundred** 有100名等待者
   a long list of 非常多的～

5. **execution of order** 訂單的履行

6. **to date, to this date** 至今

7. **the nearest to this item** 最類似的產品

8. **line**〔laɪn〕*n.* 貨品之一種
   the items of this line 此種貨品中的項目

9. **itemized statement** 分項列舉的說明書

10. **if it is within our power** 若在我方能力範圍內

11. **to do all in** *one's* **power** 盡全力

12. **as requested** 依照要求

13. **immediate shipment** 即期裝運；接受訂單後 1 個月的船運

訂　單　模　範　書　信

A. 發送訂單（ Despatch of Order ）

1

We have pleasure in sending you an order for 1,000 bales of cotton products, ***based on*** the quotations you referred to us in your letter of May 5. We have ***a large demand*** here for the same goods. Prices are to be CIF Kaohsiung. Your prompt execution will be highly appreciated.

　　根據貴方 5 月 5 日來函中所示的報價，本公司甚感榮幸為您寄上一千綑棉製品的訂單。本地對同一貨品的需求甚大。價格依到高雄的運費保險費在內價計算。如蒙即時履行，不勝感激。

➡ **CIF =** *cost , insurance & freight* 運費、保險費在內價；起岸價

B. 承諾訂單 (Acceptance of Order)

1

Thank you very much for your order of March 20 for 30 doz of Tea Services No. 53. The items are now in stock and we can guarantee delivery to your Liverpool warehouse *well before* April 10. *As requested,* we will advise you of the date of despatch. *We are at your service at all times.*

承蒙貴方於 3 月 20 日訂購 30 打第 53 號茶具，不勝感激。該品目前有存貨，本公司保證在 4 月 10 日前甚早即可送至您利物浦的倉庫。我方將依您所請，通知發送日期，並隨時為您提供服務。

➡ warehouse〔'wer͵haus〕*n.* 倉庫；大的零售商店

C. 委託代購 (Indent)

1

The goods of your last shipment are very popular in our district *enjoying ready sales* and are expected to be out of stock shortly. Such being the case, we would *renew the order for* the same goods, provided our fresh order be priced at the same limits as in the previous case which are specified in the enclosed *order sheet*. If you would agree to this, may we ask you to arrange for immediate shipment of *each lot*. We herewith enclosed a copy of our Indent *for your reference*.

　　貴方前批貨品在本區至受歡迎，廣爲暢銷，存貨預計於近日內告罄。有鑑於此，倘若我方的再購訂單能依上回的限價（已載明於附寄的訂單上）定價，本公司將再次訂購同一貨品。若獲同意，煩請您爲各批貨品安排卽期裝運。隨函附寄我方代購訂單複本一份，以資查照。

➡ lot〔lɑt〕*n.* （貨物的）一批；一堆

D. 拒絕訂單（Refusal of Order）

1

We thank you very much for the order contained in your letter of December 20. After carefully considering it, however, we have come to the conclusion that it would be better for you to approach another manufacturer *in this instance*. To machine to the limits required in your specification would require the setting up of special equipment at our works, and this would not only be impossible before September

but would seriously *interrupt our normal production.*
We are sorry not to be more helpful, but hope that
you will understand our position. Do let us have other
enquiries at any time, as we shall be only too pleased
to meet you if *it is within our power.*

(*MODERN ENGLISH BUSINESS LETTERS*)

　　承蒙貴方12月20日來函訂購，不勝感激。然而，經慎重考慮後，本公司決定，關於此事您最好與其他製造商接洽。爲了用機器製出您設計書要求之程度，我方必須在工廠中裝設特殊設備。此舉不僅無法在9月前完成，並會嚴重阻礙我方正常的生產。未能效勞，至感抱歉，但甚盼您能了解我方立場。務必隨時來函查詢，因爲若在能力範圍內，我方將樂意配合。

➡ specification〔,spɛsəfə'keʃən〕*n.* 設計書；詳細說明書

E. 取消訂單 (Cancellation of Order)

1

We are writing immediately to solicit you to cancel
our May 15 *rush order* for 50 dozen nylon stockings,
should the shipment have not yet been made to date.
To tell the truth, the *orderer* phoned to us to with-
draw his offer immediately after his placing orders
with us. If the shipment has already been effected,

we are of course ready to receive the goods of our order. We are very sorry for this trouble, which we well know will *cause* you *much inconvenience*, but we should be highly grateful if you would *be kind enough to* agree to our such request, taking our position into due consideration. Looking forward to your early reply,

若本公司5月15日緊急訂單的50打尼龍長襪至今日尚未裝運,我方請求貴方迅速取消該批訂單的貨品。事實上,訂購者在向我方訂購後,隨即電告我方撤銷其報價。倘若已經裝運,我方必當接受訂單上的貨品。此事必然帶給您諸多不便,對此麻煩至感抱歉。但若蒙適度考慮我方立場,並慨然接受我方請求,則感幸甚。期待早日回覆。

第5章
信用狀
Letter of Credit

1.開立信用狀　Opening of L/C

1. 信用狀（ Letter of Credit→簡稱 L/C 或 Credit ）

信用狀是排除遙隔兩地的出口商和進口商，對付款上的不安，使貿易順利進行的支付保證書。信用狀的當事人有進口商→開狀銀行→通知銀行→出口商，因為其中包括兩家銀行，那麼即使進口商不付款，受進口商委託的開狀銀行也要負起付款的責任，所以出口商可以安心地輸出貨物。

首先由進口商向外匯銀行提出擔保，請求銀行開狀，然後用電報或 airmail（航空郵件）通知出口商 L/C 的號碼及詳細情形。同時，開狀銀行以信件、電報或電傳等方式，將信用狀送交到出口地的**分行**或**押匯**

銀行（ **negotiating bank** ）。收到的銀行（ 通知銀行 ）再將 L/C 送達出口商 。有時由開狀銀行直接寄達出口商，但大部分還是經由通知銀行寄送 。通常若以電報傳送時，原則上要以 airmail 寄出電報確認書 。

2.信用狀的當事人（ **parties to L/C** ）

a）委託開狀人（ 進口商 ）— importer

b）開狀銀行— credit-issuing bank

c）通知銀行或通滙銀行— notifying bank or correspondent bank

d）押滙銀行— negotiating bank（ 大多由通知銀行兼任 ）

3.信用狀的主要種類

a）**不可撤銷信用狀**（ **irrevocable L/C** ）：是最普通的信用狀，內容不可變更，修改時也必須經過 L/C 全體當事人的同意 。

b）**可撤銷信用狀**（ **revocable L/C** ）：由於內容可變更，在貿易上有所顧慮，所以較少被採用 。

c）**保兌信用狀**（ **confirmed L/C** ）：是開狀銀行國際信用較低時，由出口地的通知銀行與開狀銀行雙重擔保的 L/C 。出口商不放心時也可以要求開出這種信用狀 。

開 立 信 用 狀 必 備 例 句

A. 請求開立信用狀（ **Request for Opening of L/C** ）

1. Please open by cable an irrevocable letter of ***credit for*** the

請以電報開立一張貴方…訂單,金額五千美元的

amount of $5,000 covering your order for... *in favor of* Messrs. John Smith & Co.

不可撤銷信用狀，受益人爲約翰・史密斯公司。

> ➡ irrevocable〔ɪ'rɛvəkəbl̩〕*adj.* 不可撤銷的
> ➡ *in favor of* ~ 以~爲受益人

2. We request you to *establish* by cable a letter of credit *with* Bank of Taiwan *for* the amount of $5,000.

懇請貴方以電報開給台灣銀行，金額五千元的信用狀一張。

3. The undersigned hereby requests you to issue by cable (mail) your irrevocable letter of credit as follows:

　　in favor of...（出口商）
　　for account of...（進口實需者）
　　up to the aggregate amount of...
　　available by draft drawn, at your option, on（出票人）you or any of your correspondents.

下署者在此懇請貴方依下列以電報（郵寄）開立不可撤銷信用狀：
受益人…（出口商）
付款人…（進口實需者）
總金額可達…
任君選擇，開滙票給貴方或任何一間您的通滙銀行，見票支付。

4. *With reference to* your order No. ~, we have not yet received your credit to date. The time of shipment is imminent, so you are requested to *open a credit* as soon as possible.

本公司至今尚未收到貴方第~號訂單的信用狀。船期將至，故懇請您儘速開立信用狀。

請求開發信用狀的結尾語

1. Please let us know the number of
   a credit as soon as it is opened.

   懇請於信用狀開立後，
   立卽告訴本公司其編號。

2. Immediate shipment is *guaranteed*
   upon the arrival of your L/C.

   一俟接獲貴方信用狀，
   保證立卽裝運。

   ➡ guarantee〔,gærən'ti〕 *n.* 保證；擔保

B. 開狀通知 (Advice of Opening of L/C)

1. Today we instructed Bank of Taiwan to open a credit for $ 10,000
   in your favor.

   今日本公司指示台灣銀
   行，開立一張以貴方爲
   受益人的一萬元信用狀。

2. This is to advise you that today
   we opened an *irrevocable letter
   of credit* for the amount of
   $ 10,000 *in your favor*.

   此函係通知貴方，今日
   本公司開出一張以您爲
   受益人，金額一萬元的
   不可撤銷信用狀。

3. We are pleased to inform you
   that an *irrevocable letter of
   credit* covering our order has
   been established *in your favor*.

   本公司已開立承保訂單
   的不可撤銷信用狀，以
   您爲受益人，特此奉告。

4. We hasten to advise you that with
   reference to our order No. ～, we
   are now arranging to open an

   本公司急於通知貴方，
   關於第～號訂單，我方
   正安排請台灣銀行，開

irrevocable letter of credit with Bank of Taiwan **in your favor**.

立以您爲受益人的不可撤銷信用狀。

5. This is to inform you that to cover your shipment of our order No. ～, we have established an **irrevocable letter of credit** by cable today with the National Bank of New York, **in your favor**.

本函係通知貴方，爲承保您對本公司第～號訂單船貨費，我方今天已經以您爲受益人，請紐約國民銀行，以電報開立不可撤銷信用狀。

開狀通知的結尾語

1. We look forward to your early **arrangements for** shipping our order.

盼貴方能安排我方訂貨早日裝船。

2. Please **despatch** as quickly as possible.

敬請儘速發送。

3. Upon opening of the credit, you will **be** immediately **advised of** its number.

一俟開立信用狀，即當通知貴方其編號。

2. 信用狀有效期限及修改 Validity & Amendment of L/C

L/C（**信用狀**）的有效期限是從L/C發行日起至押滙銀行押滙爲止。L/C新統一規則規定，須寫明裝船期限、有效期限，以及完成裝

船到押滙的期限（參考書末的附錄信用狀形式）。當裝船期限延長時，有效期限必然也跟著延長，這種延長修改要另行註明裝船期限、有效期限。例如，因為罷工或 L／C 遲到時，裝船延期使得 L／C 的有效期限也跟著延長。要做這種修改（ amendment ）的出口商直接以電報、電傳向進口商請求修改，進口商再向開狀銀行陳情，再傳達至通知銀行，務需獲得當事人（ parties to L/C ）全體同意才可以。若只延長有效期限而未延長裝船期限時，仍然要修改出貨期限和有效期限兩項。

L／C 的修改視情況而定，大多是出口商請求進口商修改，有時也由進口商提出變更信用狀金額，或其他不得不變更的內容。尤其是**契約內容需與 L／C 的內容一致**，但是往往會發生不一致的狀況，這時就得緊急通知修改。若 L／C 的內容有與裝船文件內容不胳合時，銀行可以拒絕押滙。

信 用 狀 有 效 期 限 及 修 改 必 備 例 句

A. 信用狀的期限與修改（ Expiry & Amendment of L／C ）

1. This credit is *to remain in force* until June 30.

   本信用狀將持續至 6 月 30 日有效。

2. This credit *expires on* June 30, 1986 in the country of the *beneficiary* for negotiation.

   本信用狀將於 1986 年 6 月 30 日，在受益人所在國期滿押滙。

   ➡ beneficiary〔͵bɛnəˋfɪʃɪrɪ〕*n.* 受益人

   ➡ negotiation〔nɪ͵goʃɪˋeʃən〕*n.* 押滙；議付

3. *You are kindly advised that* our letter of credit No. 8790 has been *extended to* March 19.

我方第 8790 號信用狀已延期至 3 月19日，特此奉告。

4. May we ask you for a two-week extension of the *validity* of our irrevocable letter of credit No. ～ issued by Bank of Taiwan? The reason is that....

能否懇請貴方准予本公司，由台灣銀行開出的第～號不可撤銷信用狀之有效期限延緩兩週？原因爲… 。

➡ validity〔vəˈlɪdətɪ〕*n*. 有效期限

5. We hasten to request you to *amend* our letter of credit No. ～ as follows:

本公司急於懇請貴方修改第～號信用狀如下：

修改信用狀有效期限的結尾語

1. As this is the case, please accept our request for *extension* of the credit.

有鑑於此，敬請接受本公司要求信用狀延期之請。

2. Your *prompt attention to* this would be greatly appreciated.

如蒙卽時處理此案，不勝感激。

3. Under such circumstances, we would request you to *amend* the L/C No. 500 by cable.

於此情形下，懇請貴方以電報修改第 500 號信用狀。

4. We should be much obliged if you would agree to our request for *amendment*.

如同意我方修改的請求，則不勝感激。

B. 請求修改信用狀之囘覆 (Reply to Request for Amendment to L/C)

1. We have received your letter asking for *a two-week extension* of Bank of Taiwan's irrevocable L/C No. ~.

貴方要求對台灣銀行第～號不可撤銷信用狀延期兩週的來函，業已收到。

2. Your request for two-week extension of your irrevocable credit No. ~ has been received. *As the matter stands*, we cannot but agree to the *proposed* extension.

貴方要求將第～號信用狀延期二週的來函，業已收到。依現況，我方不得不同意所請。

3. Your request for *amendment to* your irrevocable credit No. ~ has been accepted.

貴方要求修改第～號不可撤銷信用狀，已獲接受。

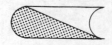 信 用 狀 須 知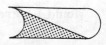

1. 一般貿易都由**代理人**(agent)充當進口商和出口商，但是背後還有實際的進口人和出口人。若出口人是廠商，且廠商又兼作貿易商時，稱爲廠商的**直接貿易**。貿易公司是進出口人的 agent。實際進

口人稱爲實需者，進口費用應由此實需者支付。常用 **for account of ～**，意思爲〔付款人爲××實需者〕。

2. to **issue**（**open, establish**）an L/C **with** × **Bank in favor of** A（exporter 爲 beneficiary）

　　請×銀行開立一張以出口商A爲受益人的信用狀。

3. **for account of** B（importer）

　　付款人爲B進口商；由進口商支付

4. beneficiary〔,bɛnə'fɪʃərɪ〕*n.* 受益人；出口商。亦即藉由出口而獲利的人。

5. **in** *one's* **favor** 以～爲受益人或抬頭人

6. **notifying bank** 通知銀行；**correspondent bank** 通滙銀行

7. **negotiating bank** 押滙銀行；滙票議付銀行

8. **negotiate**〔nɪ'goʃɪ,et〕*v.* 押滙；將滙票兌換成現金
　　名詞爲 **negotiation**,非「交涉」之意。

9. **term of credit**（**validity**）L/C 的有效期限

10. **expiry date** 期滿日期

信 用 狀 模 範 書 信

A. 信用狀（Letter of Credit）

1

Today we *opened* by cable an irrevocable letter of credit No. 1567 *covering* our order for 10 DIESEL MOTORS *with* the Bank of America in Taipei.

今日本公司請台北的美國商業銀行，以電報開立第1567號不可撤銷信用狀，以承保我方訂購的十台柴油機。

➡ diesel motor〔engine〕柴油機

2

We have received your cable of May 5 asking for the opening of an *irrevocable letter of credit* covering our order No. 156 for 100 bales of cotton products. As requested, we today *established an irrevocable credit* No. 1890 *in your favor with* the National Bank of New York, N.Y., *for* US$ 10,000 covering our order. We should be grateful if you would arrange for prompt shipment.

　　貴方於 5 月 5 日電報要求本公司，開立不可撤銷信用狀，以承保一百綑棉製品的第 156 號訂單，業已收到。我方今日依所求，請紐約州的紐約國民銀行，開立以您為受益人，訂單金額美金一萬元，第 1890 號不可撤銷信用狀，如蒙安排即期裝運，則感幸甚。

3

Your letter of credit covering your order No. 10 of September 25 has not yet reached us to date. As the shipping time is imminent, please *open by cable* immediately.

　　貴方 9 月 25 日第 10 號訂單的信用狀，本公司至今尚未收到。由於船期迫近，敬請迅即以電報開立。

4

We hasten to advise you that the shipment of 100 units of LADY'S SPORTS CYCLE *on your order* of May 10 has been called off due to the June typhoon. The cargo was originally scheduled to be shipped to Bombay by s.s. "President" sailing from Keelung on July 20. Weathermen say, however, that the typhoon may leave in about 5 days, and we would ask you to

> immediately arrange for the *extension of L/C ship-*
> *ment and validity for* **10** *days respectively*.

　本公司緊急通知貴方，由於麥恩颱風的關係，您 5 月 10 日訂購的一百台女用運動自行車船期已經取消。該批貨品原訂在 7 月 20 日從基隆啟航的總統號輪載往孟買。不過，氣象人員認為颱風約在五天內離境，因而我方恭請您立即安排，將信用狀的裝船期限與有效期限分別延長十天。

➡ cargo〔ˈkɑrgo〕*n*.（船、飛機等所載的）貨物

➡ schedule〔ˈskɛdʒʊl〕*v*. 排定；列入時間表中

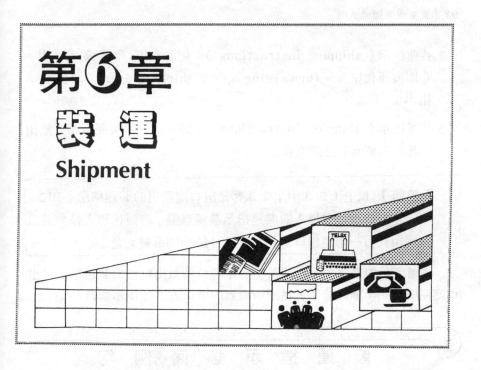

第6章 裝運
Shipment

1. 裝運指示　Shipping Instructions

　　與國外貿易時，進出口商在成立買賣契約後，進口商得向國貿局提出輸入許可證申請書，完成進口手續。然後要寄送**裝運指示**（ shipping instruction ）給出口商，並附寄**嘜頭**（ shipping mark ）以及裝運貨名、包裝方式、目的港、裝船日期、運輸條件（ **CIF、FOB**等）等主要項目。裝運指示和普通文件形式並無不同，但是要條列各必要事項。本章裝運指示指的是進口商寄給出口商的文件，千萬不要與下列文件混淆：

1. 裝運單（ shipping order，S／O ）：船公司致租船船長，指示裝運的文件。

2.裝運指示（ shipping instructions ）：這種是出口商致船務業者
（即海運代理人— forwarding agent, shipping agent）的裝運
指示。

3.裝運指示（ shipping instructions ）：這是另一種裝運指示，爲出
口商指示廠商裝運的文件。

> 【 說明 】 以上 1. 2. 3. 中，2. 3. 都是出口商發出的裝運指示。如 2.
> 這種致海運代理人的裝運指示最爲普遍。海運代理人替貿易公
> 司代行一切進出口實務，是不可缺少的重要角色。

本章所提的裝運指示不同於上，是進口商致出口商的裝運指示，出
口商完成海關手續之後，就按照所收到的進口商裝運指示進行裝船。

裝 運 指 示 必 備 例 句

A. 出口商→進口商（ Exporter → Importer ）

1. As to your goods, we have finished
   customs formalities, and are waiting for your shipping instructions.

   關於貴方貨品，本公司
   已完成海關手續，正恭
   候您的裝運指示。

   ➡ formality〔 fɔrˊmælətɪ 〕*n.*(*pl.*) 正規的手續

2. *Acting upon* shipping instructions
   included in your letter of March
   10, we shipped your order *on the
   s.s.* "*Universe*" sailing from
   Keelung on April 1.

   遵照貴方3月10日來函
   中的裝運指示，訂貨已
   由宇宙輪載運，於4月
   1日從基隆啟航。

3. As we are ready for shipment,
   we hope you will send us *marks*
   and *shipping instructions*.

由於本公司已備妥裝運，
盼貴方寄來嘜頭與裝運
指示。

4. We hope you will *forward* immediately the necessary instructions
   as to the shipment and these will
   have our attention *in due course*.

盼貴方即時轉寄有關裝
運的必要指示，以使本
公司適時處理。

→ forward〔ˈfɔrwəd〕*v.* 轉寄；運送
→ *in due course* 到適當的時候；照自然的發展順序

5. The goods of your order No. 567
   are *packed* and ready for *despatch*
   and we shall be pleased if you
   will *fill up,* sign, and return the
   attached *instructions form* as
   soon as possible.

貴方第567號訂單的貨
品已包裝妥當準備發送。
若蒙您儘速填妥、簽署
並寄回隨信附寄的指示
表格，則感幸甚。

→ *fill up* 填妥；裝滿

6. Your instructions have been noted
   and we will collect the parcel for
   despatch by *the next available
   vessel*.

貴方的指示已敬悉，本
公司將備妥貨品，俟下
次船期即可發送。

B. 進口商→出口商（ Importer → Exporter ）

1. The goods to be forwarded *per*
   EVERGREEN LINE steamer from

貨品將由長榮航運的輪
船由基隆運至新加坡。

Keelung to Singapore. *Shipping Advice* to be sent to us *direct*.

請將裝船通知直接寄給本公司。

→ steamer〔'stimə〕*n.* 輪船；汽船
→ shipping advice 裝運通知

2. Packages should be marked and numbered, *as per* shipping instructions.

包裝應按裝運指示印上嘜頭並編號。

→ *as per* 按；照

3. We thank you for your letter of October 1 and we now return your shipping instructions form *duly completed*, *with* 2 copies of commercial invoice *attached*.

貴方10月1日來函敬悉。本公司現在將填妥之裝運指示表寄回，隨函附寄兩份商業發票。

→ invoice〔'ɪnvɔɪs〕*n.* 發票

4. With regard to the shipment of our order TK—250 covering the *undermentioned* goods, please *observe* the following terms and conditions:
   Star Printing Press Model DG—5 30 units @ $ 4,000 FOB SAN FRANCISCO per unit.
   1. Be sure to *pack* each in

關於本公司TK—250號訂單的下列貨品，敬請遵守以下條件裝運：
　　星星印刷機DG—5型30台
　　每台到舊金山船上交貨價四千元。
　　1.務請每台均以堅固木箱包裝。
　　2.嘜頭如下：

one strong wooden case.

2. ***Shipping mark*** to be given
   as follows:

3. Shipment to be made by
   April 15, 1986.

4. When shipment is effected,
   please telex us immediately
   stating:

Name and No. of ***shipped cargo***,
No. of B/L, Gross weight of
package, Total invoice amount.
This telex message is very important and will save so much
time for ***Customs Clearance***.
Your special attention to this
will be highly appreciated.

➡ FOB = *free on board* 船上交貨價；離岸價
➡ B/L = *bill of lading* 提單
➡ customs clearance 報關

3. 請於 1986年4月
   15日前裝船。

4. 當船運完成，請
   立即電傳告知我
   方：

裝運貨品名稱及
編號、提單號碼、
貨品毛重，發票
總額。

此電傳電文至關
緊要，可省去甚
多報關時間。

若承蒙您特別關照此事，
不勝感激。

2.裝運通知　Shipping Advice

　　出口商在接到進口商寄來的裝運指示和信用狀後，就必須及早準備裝運事宜。首先要向船公司**洽訂船位**（ space-booking ），再將貨物搬運至**保稅區**（ bonded area ），向海關提呈**出口申請書**（ export permit ），獲得出口許可證就算完成了海關手續。等船公司簽發的**裝運單**（ **Shipping Order,** 簡稱 S/O ）一到，就開始裝船。完成裝船後，可以領到租船大副所簽發的**大副收據**（ Mate's Receipt, 簡稱M/R ），再逐向船公司換取**提單**（ **Bill of Lading,** 簡稱B/L ）。

　　這個時候，出口商通常以電傳發給進口商**裝運通知**（ shipping advice 或 shipping notice ），內容包括裝運貨品的名稱、數量、船名和**啟航日期**。這是出口商無可旁貸的義務，進口商則可據此了解船期，並推算出貨物抵達的大約日期，所以是不可缺少的商務程序之一。

　　發出裝運通知之後，出口商可持**裝運文件**（ shipping documents ）併信用狀，逐向押滙銀行（ 或原本的通知銀行 ），開出一張以信用狀上所記載的匯票付款人為抬頭的匯票，並由押滙銀行購入匯票。然後還得以航空郵件，寄裝運通知的確認書（ confirmation letter ）給進口商，內容為貨品、名稱、數量、船名、啟航日期、金額，而且要寫下「已由我方開出匯票，若收到銀行的提示，請即付款」的字樣。此外還得附寄裝船文件中心的發票（ invoice ）、B/L、保險單（ insurance policy ）等副本。

裝 運 通 知 必 備 例 句

A. 裝運指示——確認書（ Shipping Advice —Confirmation Letter ）

> 【 說明 】 裝運指示首先都是以電傳拍發，再以確認書確定，以下列舉的是確認書的例子。

1. We are pleased to inform you that your order No. 125 covering 100 bales of cotton products has been shipped on s.s. "President " of the Evergreen Line leaving Keelung on March 17 *as telexed below* :
100 BALES COTTON PRODUCTS YOUR ORDER NO. 125 SHIPPED BY PRESIDENT LEAVING KEELUNG MARCH 17.

貴方第125號訂單的一百綑棉製品，已裝運在將於3月17日由基隆啟航的長榮航運總統號輪，特此奉告。電傳如下：貴方第125號訂單的一百綑棉製品，由總統號輪承運，將於3月17日載離基隆港。

2. This is to *confirm* our March 16 telex message advising you that we have shipped your order No. 125 covering 100 bales of cotton products on s.s. "President "which left Keelung for *your destination* on the following day. We enclose copies of invoice, bill of lading and insurance policy.

本函係確認本公司3月16日的電傳電文，告知貴方第125號訂單的一百綑棉製品，已於次日由總統號輪載離基隆，駛往貴地。隨函奉寄發票、提單與保險單副本。

3. It is with pleasure that we advise you, *as per* telexed on March 16, of the *despatch* of your order No. 125 covering 100 bales of cotton products by s.s. "President" of the Evergreen Line leaving Keelung on the following day. Enclosed are copies of the *shipping documents* covering this order.

照 3 月 16 日的電傳，您第 125 號訂單的一百綑棉製品，已於次日由長榮航運的總統號輪載離基隆，特此奉告。隨函奉寄本訂單的裝運文件副本。

4. *To cover this shipment*, we have *drawn* on you at sight for $10,000 through Bank of Taiwan, Taipei. We hope you would *honor the draft* upon presentation.

爲支付此次貨運費，本公司已經由台北的台灣銀行，開出以貴方爲抬頭的一萬元即期滙票，盼您在提示時承兌本滙票。

➡ honor〔'ɑnɚ〕 *v*. 承兌；如期支付

5. *Against this shipment*, we have *valued* on you at 30 d/s for the amount of the enclosed invoice $10,000, through Bank of Taiwan, Taipei, which you will kindly *protect* upon presentation.

爲支付此次貨運費，本公司已經由台北的台灣銀行，以貴方爲抬頭，開立附寄的發票金額一萬元、見票三十天後付款的滙票，請貴方在提示時，予以承兌。

➡ d/s = *day's sight*；*days after sight* 見票後～天付款
➡ protect〔prə'tɛkt〕 *v*. 承兌；準備支付金

裝運指示的結尾語

1. We trust that the goods *will be found in order* upon arrival and will meet with your approval.

   ➡ *in order* 安然地

   本公司相信在貨物抵達時，您會發現一切安然無損，並感到滿意。

2. We trust that the goods will arrive *in excellent condition* and that their quality will *induce* you to entrust us with further commands.

   ➡ *in excellent* (*good*) *condition* （指東西）完好無瑕疵

   ➡ entrust〔ɪn'trʌst〕 *v*. 委託；託付

   相信貨品抵達時，將完好而無瑕疵，且其品質將促使貴方惠賜更多訂單。

3. We trust this shipment will reach you safely and *in good condition*.

   相信這批貨將安然完好抵達貴處。

4. The *consignment*, we feel sure, will arrive *in good condition* and prove entirely satisfactory.

   ➡ consignment〔kən'saɪnmənt〕 *n*. 託售貨物

   相信該託售貨物將完好抵達，並使貴方完全滿意。

5. The goods, we trust, will arrive *in time* and meet with your approval.

   深信此批貨品將及時抵達，並可令貴方滿意。

6. We trust that the goods of your
   order will reach you *in good condition*
   and give you perfect satisfaction.

相信貴方訂購的貨品將完好抵達，並令您完全滿意。

7. We trust that the goods will
   come to hand in good order and
   that you will find them *suitable*
   for your purpose.

本公司相信該貨品將完好抵達，並切合貴方需要。

➡ *come to hand* 收到；到手

B. 船貨抵達（ Arrival of Shipment ）

1. Today we received your *shipment*
   of our order No. ～.

貴方發送的本公司第～號訂單的船貨，已於今日收到。

2. A *consignment* of 100 bales of
   cotton products on our order
   reached us today in good condition. The *checking* of *the arrivals against your invoice* has
   proved satisfactory *to our best
   thanks*.

本公司所訂購之一百綑託售棉製品今日完好抵達。到貨與貴方發票經查核無誤，至為感謝。

➡ bale〔bel〕*n.*（貨物的）綑；包

3. With many thanks we received and
   accepted today the *delivery* of
   your shipment of our order No.

貴方發送的本公司第～號訂單的船貨，已於今日抵達並已收貨，不勝

~ . The goods have arrived in good condition, proving satisfactory *to our thanks*.

感激。貨品完好抵達，深獲我方滿意，於此謹表謝忱。

4. We hasten to advise you of our *acceptance of the delivery* of your shipment in perfect condition.

貴方船貨安然無損抵達，已經收貨，並立即通知貴方。

貨物抵達的結尾語

1. We thank you again for your speedy and safe delivery.

對貴方迅速安全的交貨，本公司再致謝忱。

2. Please accept our *best thanks* for your safe delivery.

對於貴方安妥的交貨，不勝感激。

C. 未抵、有瑕疵（ **Non-Arrival ; Arrival in Bad Condition** ）

1. Your shipment of our order has not yet reached us *up to date*.

本公司訂購的貨品至今尚未抵達。

2. A consignment of cotton products *on* our order has not yet reached us *to this date* (*or*, *at the moment*, *at this writing*).

本公司所訂購的一批託售棉製品，至今（或此刻、此時）尚未抵達。

➡ *at the moment* 此刻；就在此時

3. We have not yet received your shipment of our order *at this moment*.

本公司此刻尚未收到貴方發送的我方訂購的船貨。

4. *At this writing* we *are still without* the goods of our order.

此時本公司仍未接到訂購的貨品。

5. The goods have arrived in bad condition, *proving defective and unsalable* (useless).

貨品抵達時狀況不佳，有瑕疵無法銷售（無用）。

6. The goods of our order have arrived in a damaged condition *apparently through* careless packing.

本公司所訂購貨品抵達時已受損，顯然因包裝不慎所致。

未抵、有瑕疵的結尾語

1. Looking forward to your prompt reply,

期待貴方即時回覆。

2. We request you to *make* prompt shipment, as the goods are *urgently* needed.

由於急需此批貨品，故懇請貴方即期裝運。

3. Unless the goods can be delivered by 〔date〕, we shall have to *cancel the contract*.

除非能於〔日期〕前交貨，否則本公司將必須取消此合約。

4. We await your prompt instructions *in this instance.*

恭候貴方對此事速作指示。

5. We hasten to advise you of the *mishap* and look forward to your prompt instructions *in this instance.*

本公司緊急通知貴方此一不幸事件，並盼您對此事速作指示。

D. 出口商→進口商（ Exporter → Importer ）

1. We are really sorry for the delay in shipment caused by ... 〔the *docker' strike*; the goods ordered *running out of* stock〕.

由於…〔碼頭工人罷工；所訂貨品存貨售罄〕，以致延遲裝運，至感抱歉。

→ docker 〔'dɑkə〕 *n.* 碼頭工人
→ *run out of* 用光；(缺)貨

2. We have *duly* received your letter requesting the early delivery of your order.

貴方要求早日運送您的訂貨的來函，已適時收到。

3. We deeply apologize for the *delay in* the *shipment* of your order.

延誤裝運貴方的訂貨，本公司至感抱歉。

出口商→進口商的結尾語

1. We *assure* you that the goods will be delivered to you within a week.

本公司保證將於一週內交貨。

2. We should be very grateful if you
would be kind enough to grant us
a few days' grace for shipment,
taking into due consideration the
circumstances we are placed in.

如蒙貴方好意適度考慮
本公司處境，而准予寬
限數日裝船，則感幸甚。

→ grace〔gres〕*n*. 寬限；緩期

E. 變更裝運日期（ Change of Shipping Schedule ）

1. We regret that the shipment of
your order has been *put off* till
May as we found no April vessel
available for New York.

至感抱歉，由於本公司
無法覓得於4月駛往紐
約的船隻，貴方訂貨的
裝運已延至5月。

2. The Dinah typhoon has *tied up* all
cargo work, *resulting in* the ten-
days' postponement of *lay days*.

黛納颱風已使所有貨運
工作中斷，致使裝貨時
間延長十日。

→ *tie up* 使中斷；使動彈不得
→ lay days 裝貨或卸貨時間；停泊期間

3. Owing to the manufacturers' production delay, we have *missed* the
February shipment and loaded your
order *on the first avaliable March
service* for your destination.
Please forgive our action considering the circumstances we are placed in.

由於製造商生產上的延
遲，本公司錯過2月船
期，並將貴方訂貨裝於
3月駛往貴地的第一艘
船隻。請考慮我方處境，
而寬恕此措施。

4. Shipment has been delayed one week till July 10 from July 3 *originally scheduled*, due to the Nelson typhoon *tying up* the vessel in port *as many* days.

由於尼爾森颱風，使得船隻停泊在港一週，因而船運由原訂的 7 月 3 日延後一週至 7 月 10 日。

→ originally 〔 ə′rɪdʒənəlɪ 〕*adv*. 原來地；最初地

5. We deeply apologize（We are really sorry）for the delay in shipment due to the holidays of the Chinese New Year.

本公司對由於春節假期而造成的裝運延誤，至感抱歉。

6. We hasten to advise you that the shipment of your order has been *suspended due to* the Andy typhoon, which, however, is reported to leave in some five days. So may we ask you to extend *L/C shipment and expiry* for 10 days respectively?

本公司緊急通知貴方，由於安迪颱風，您的訂貨已暫停裝船。不過，此颱風據報將於五天左右離境。因而可否請您將信用狀的裝船期限，與有效期限分別延長十日？

→ suspend 〔 sə′spɛnd 〕*v*. 暫時停止

F. 分批裝運（Partial Shipment）

1. It is to our deep regret that we cannot *send your order in full* as the goods *in question* are almost

由於所提到的貨品存貨幾已用罄，本公司至感遺憾，無法將貴方的訂

running out of stock, and may we despatch the goods now *on hand* immediately and, for the rest, to await for ten days as we will make a fresh order at once *with* the manufacturer?

貨全數送上。因此我方可否先將現貨卽期發送，餘額則暫候十日，我方將立卽與製造商下再購訂單？

➡ *in full* 全數的；全額的

➡ *in question* 議論中的；正被討論的

2. We have just received your credit and *are sending* your order *in two lots*, *viz* March/April shipment, as the credit permits *partial shipment*.

本公司適才接獲貴方信用狀，由於狀上允許分批裝運，因而將把您的訂貨分爲3月與4月兩批裝運。

➡ lot〔lɑt〕*n.* （貨物的）一批

➡ viz〔vɪz〕卽；就是

3. We regret that your order cannot be shipped *in one lot* as the steamer has not enough space for *shipment in full* due to freight congestion. Such being the case, we would despatch the *remainder* by the earliest available next vessel, which you will kindly *acknowledge*.

本公司至感遺憾地通知貴方，由於貨物擁擠，輪船無足夠艙位載運全數貨品，因而您的訂貨無法整批裝運。有鑑於此，我方將利用下班最早的船次，發送剩餘的貨品。敬請首肯。

➡ congestion〔kən'dʒɛstʃən〕*n.* 充滿；擁擠

4. It is to our regret to have to inform you that the manufacturer's production delay makes it impossible for us to *despatch your order in full*. At present we have only 30 packages of the brands named and would you *grant us a two-week grace* for the shipment of the whole lots as the letter of credit does not permit *partial shipment*?

本公司至感遺憾必須通知您，由於製造商生產延誤，我方無法全數發送您的訂貨。目前我方只有三十箱指定商標的產品，由於信用狀不允許分批裝運，故可否寬限兩週，以便整批裝運？

G. 轉運（ Transshipment ）

1. *The goods of the "President"* have been *transshipped into* the s.s. "Perilus" *at* Bombay.

總統號輪上的貨品，已在孟買由帕利勒斯號轉運。

➡ transship〔 træns'ʃɪp 〕*v.* 轉運；轉船

2. The silk goods for Boston will be transshipped *at* New York *by rail*.

運往波士頓的絲製品，將在紐約港由火車轉運。

3. May we ask you to take the trouble of *quoting us CIF San Jose prices* henceforth *on a dual basis* ...for *shipment* by a direct

能否麻煩貴方今後依雙重基礎──由直達輪船裝運，並在美國太平洋岸港口轉運──給本公

steamer and ***with*** the transshipment at US Pacific coast ports?

> dual〔'duəl〕*adj.* 雙重的；二元的

司到聖約瑟運費、保險
費在內的報價？

4. The goods can be forwarded to
the destination by ***a through bill
of lading*** with the transshipment
at Singapore.

> through bill of lading 聯運提單

貨品可在新加坡轉船，
藉聯運提單轉運至目的
地。

5. The transshipment ***en route*** will
affect the early delivery of the
goods.

> ***en route***〔an'rut〕在途中

中途轉運將影響貨品的
早日交貨。

6. Please arrange to ***transship*** at
Singapore the goods on the
"President" ***on board*** a vessel
for Bombay, the port of destination, ***booking the space*** on your
side, since the Chinese steamer
sails direct for Jakarta.

> book〔bʊk〕*v.* 洽訂；登記

煩請在新加坡安排一艘
駛往目的地港─孟買的
船隻，並請貴方洽訂船
位，以轉運總統號輪船
上的貨物，因為該中國
輪船直航雅加達。

7. As the cargo is to be transshipped at Singapore, we shall
require ***through B/L***.

由於貨物預定於新加坡
轉運，本公司將需要聯
運提單。

H. 短裝；超裝（ Short shipment；Overshipment ）

1. Unfortunately, three of 50 cases of your order No. 567 were **shut out** at Keelung owing to a **clercial mistake** on our part, for which we deeply apologize. The **short-shipped goods** will be despatched immediately by the next steamer.

   ➡ **shut out** 退關

   由於本公司抄寫上的錯誤，貴方第 567 號訂單上的五十箱中，有三箱不幸在基隆被退關，我方至感抱歉。短裝的貨品將立卽由下班輪船發送。

2. Upon checking **the arrivals against** the invoice, we found that there was **an over-shipment** of three cartons of Manila-produced cigars on our order. Of course, we are ready to send **the overage** back to you, but advise us how to handle this matter. Looking forward to your instructions,

   ➡ overage〔 ′ovərɪdʒ 〕 *n.* （商品）過賸

   當本公司憑發票核對到貨時，發現較我方訂單多運了三紙盒馬尼拉雪茄。我方當然準備將多餘貨品寄回，但請告知如何處理此事。亟盼貴方指示。

3. A considerable number of soybean-contained linen bags were **left off** at the station platform as their arrival was a little late for train departure.

   ➡ soybean〔′sɔɪ′bin 〕 *n.* 大豆；黃豆

   由於貨到時火車已開，故有相當多裝有大豆的麻袋，被留在車站的月台上。

4. Your shipment has arrived, but a check-up has revealed a *shortage* (*an overage*) of three packs of orange *for the invoiced volume*.

貴方船貨已送達，但是檢查後發現較發票的數量短少（多出）三箱柳丁。

➡ volume〔ˊvɑljəm〕*n.* 數量；總額

5. Numerous cases of *over-and-under-shipment* of cargo took place *in the wake of* the Anita typhoon.

繼安妮塔颱風之後，發生了多起超裝和短裝貨物的事件。

➡ *in the wake of* 繼…之後

6. In reply to your telex of March 10 informing us of the shortage of two parcels, we immediately sent out *tracers* to the quarters concerned to find that the goods *in question* were *overcarried* and landed at Colombo by mistake. We are now making arrangements to have the goods returned to Bombay *by the first available opportunity*.

答覆貴方3月10日告知短少兩包貨品的電傳，本公司立即將貨物追查狀寄給有關方面，結果發現提及的貨品係超載，並誤在可倫坡卸貨。我方目前正安排利用最近之船次，將貨品送還至孟買。

➡ tracer〔ˊtresə〕*n.* 追查狀
➡ quarter〔ˊkwɔrtə〕*n.* 方面；（消息等的）來源

I. 裝貨、或卸貨港口的檢驗 (Inspection at Shipping or Landed Port)

1. We have inspected the *arrival casks* one by one and found that each of them leaks more or less, proving *defective and useless*. We look forward to your prompt instructions.

   ➡ cask〔kæsk〕*n.* (裝液體的)桶

   本公司一一檢驗到貨的桶子，發現每只均或多或少有漏洞，顯示有瑕疵而無用，亟盼貴方卽時指示。

2. We were suprised *at your complaint* that the quality of our shipment has changed considerably upon arrival. The goods were carefully inspected and analyzed *at loading.* If the change of quality is *the actual case*, it must have come from the change in temperature during the long voyage.

   得知貴方抱怨本公司貨品運抵時，品質變化甚多，我方至感驚訝。該批貨品於裝載時均經仔細檢驗與分析。若品質果真產生變化，必因長途航行中的溫度變化所致。

3. The Agreement says that *"Inspection at loading to be taken as final,"* and Article 11 of the Agreement on General Terms And Conditions stipulates that A shall ship all goods *in good condition*

   契約中說：「以裝載時的檢驗爲最終條件」而契約中有關一般條件的第十一條規定：「Ａ方必須將所有貨品完整無缺地裝船，而Ｂ方必須

and B shall *assume* all risks of damage, deterioration, or breakage during transportation.

承擔運輸途中一切損壞、變質或破損的風險。」

➡ stipulate〔'stɪpjə,let〕*v.* 規定

➡ deterioration〔dɪ,tɪrɪə'reʃən〕*n.* 變質；變壞

4. Therefore we feel it a great regret to have to conclude that we have no responsibility for the *deterioration* of the quality *in transit* nor do we have the right of *compensation* for the damage.

因此，本公司甚爲遺憾地斷定，我方對運輸途中的變質沒有責任，亦無賠償損害的義務。

➡ transit〔'trænsɪt〕*n.* 運輸；搬運

裝貨、或卸貨港口的檢驗結尾語

1. However, we cannot but feel great sympathy towards the mishap you have suffered *in this instance*, and *for your next possible order*, we are ready to offer you a 5 percent *cut* in the whole price. *Soliciting* your understanding of our position and looking forward to the continuance of your favor,

無論如何，本公司對貴方於此案，所遭受的不幸不得不至感同情。如可能再獲貴方訂單，我方準備提供您低於總價百分之五的報價。懇請您諒解我方立場，並盼繼續關愛支持。

➡ solicit〔sə'lɪsɪt〕*v.* 懇求

2. As regards the quality of goods, *the landed analysis* is to be *taken as final*. Should the quality at the destination be found *inferior to* that at the shipping port, the shipper is to offer the *consignee* a reasonable discount of the price thereof.

關於貨物品質，將以卸貨分析爲最終條件。倘若到目的地時，品質較在裝運港口差，將由裝運人提供收貨人相關價格的合理折扣。

➡ consignee 〔 ,kɑnsaɪ′ni 〕 *n.* 收貨人；承銷人

3.貨櫃輸送 Container Transport

比起傳統船運的逐項嚴密包裝裝船，以及在船艙或甲板裝運**散裝貨**（ bulk cargo ），能夠裝運於貨櫃中的物品，若完全以貨櫃方式處理，不但較易移動，也可節省許多卸貨時間及包裝費用。

這種能堪反覆運輸，近代文明下的堅實運輸容器，很容易轉運，且能達到**海陸聯運**（ Land Bridge ）的目的。甚至配合近年來的巨型運輸機，而達到**海陸空三位一體的聯運**（ Round Bridge ）。由於**海運貨櫃化**（ containerization ）的緣故，幾條主要航線幾乎全由貨櫃船取代傳統的貨船。又因為貨櫃在裝船時，可以在甲板上重疊兩、三層，而節約了大量的空間（ space ）。

先用大型起重機，把裝在拖車上的貨櫃，移到活動扶梯，稱為ramp（ 結合船身和陸地的橋樑— gangway ），再以堆高機（ forklift ）裝運。因此，卸貨時手續就大為簡易，並節省勞力，甚而造成碼頭工人失業的狀況。

在貨櫃船當中有以高速著稱的full container ship（貨櫃專用船），和semi-container ship（將傳統式船艙的一部分，移作裝載之用）。通常都是藉現代化的快速貨櫃專用船載運。貨櫃碼頭（ container terminal ）是貨櫃船的起航港（ container port ），緊瀕海岸。這兒有貨櫃進出的廣大用地，即所謂的貨櫃堆場（ container yard — CY ），也就是full container load cargo（ 整櫃裝運貨物，簡稱FCL或CL cargo ）交割的場所。在CY中還有container freight station（貨櫃貨運站，簡稱CFS ），未能裝滿一箱的貨物（ less-than-container load cargo — LCL cargo ），可與其他貨物合併裝運。CL貨物由shipper（ 裝運人 ）裝船，LCL貨物則由船公司進行**合裝作業**（ consolidation ）。

在 CY 或 CFS 交付貨物時，貨主會領到 **dock receipt**（**碼頭收據**，**D/R**），這與一般貨船裝運時所領到的**大副收據**（**M/R**）一樣。等到貨櫃完全裝入貨櫃船的時候，就可以領到 container shipped B/L（貨櫃裝運提單）。

貨櫃運輸的裝運通知，除了把貨船改成貨櫃船，把港名改成貨櫃碼頭，其餘都與 2 的裝運通知相同。

貨 櫃 輸 送 必 備 例 句

1. Many thanks for your *shipping instructions* form duly completed as well as for the Letter of Credit. Upon receipt of your instructions, we immediately *got in touch with consolidators* to meet your requirements. Fortunately, we could *book a space on* the C/S "Universe" sailing from Kaohsiung Container Terminal for your destination on March 10. The despatch of cargo will be immediately advised by telex.

萬分感謝貴方適時填妥的裝運指示表及信用狀。一接獲貴方指示，本公司迅卽與合裝作業者連絡，以滿足您的需要。至爲幸運，我方在卽將於 3 月 10 日，從高雄貨櫃碼頭駛往貴地的宇宙號貨櫃輪上，洽訂到船位。貨物發送時將立卽以電傳通知。

➡ consolidator〔kən'sɑlə,detə〕*n.* 合裝作業者

2. The ***containerization*** of cargo transport by sea has developed "land bridge" —— international combined transport —— since it sharply reduces the time needed for transshipment ***en route*** facilitating inter-continental through traffic by the combination of ***container ships*** and ***container unit trains***.

海運貨物運輸的貨櫃化，已發展成「海陸聯運方式」——國際聯合運輸。因爲它顯著減少了運送途中轉運所需的時間，並藉著貨櫃船與貨櫃專用火車的聯合，而便利了洲際的直達交通。

➡ containerization〔kən,tenərə'zeʃən〕*n.* 貨櫃運輸
➡ facilitate〔fə'sɪlə,tet〕*v.* 使便利
➡ inter-continental〔,ɪntɚ,kɑntə'nɛntḷ〕*adj.* 洲際的

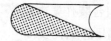 裝 運 須 知

1. **lay days**（**lay time**）（船舶之）載運或卸貨期間；停泊期間（詳情參閱下一章租船契約）

2. **containerization** 貨物運輸的貨櫃化。裝貨物於大貨櫃中，再裝運至特別製造的貨櫃專用船（ full container ship ）的甲板上，其與傳統船運相比好處極多。首先，它大量縮短了裝卸貨時間，顯著提昇了船舶的工作效率。同時可在甲板上疊裝兩、三層，又能簡化包裝，縮短轉運（ transshipment ）時間，還能達到海陸一貫運輸的目的。

3. **land bridge, round bridge** 隨著貨櫃化運輸的普及，俾能實現國際聯合運輸（ international combined transport ），即達到海陸與

陸海空聯合運輸（door-to-door transport）的可能，前者就稱為 land bridge，後者則稱為 round bridge。

a) **land bridge** （北美線）

台灣 $\xrightarrow{\text{貨櫃船}}$ 北美太平洋岸 $\xrightarrow{\text{貨櫃專用火車}}$ 北美大西洋岸

$\xrightarrow{\text{貨櫃船}}$ 歐洲

b) **round bridge** （北美線）

台灣 $\xrightarrow{\text{貨櫃船}}$ 北美太平洋岸 $\xrightarrow[\text{（橫越北美）}]{\text{飛 機}}$ $\xrightarrow{\text{貨櫃專用火車}}$

歐洲內陸

4. **Boat Note** （B/N） 交貨紀錄；這是與裝船時簽發的Mate's Receipt（大副收據，M/R）相對的文件。當貨物抵達進口港時，收貨人要清點卸下貨物的數量及其他檢查項目，然後領取船公司簽發的「卸貨單」。船公司在裝船時簽發的M/R，和卸貨時簽下的B/N，乃顯示船公司前後的責任界限，都是非常重要的文件。

5. **short-shipment , undershipment** 短裝；短貨

6. **overshipment** （動詞→ overship ） 超裝；多裝貨

7. **overage , overshipped cargo** 過謄的貨物

8. **shortage , short-landed cargo** 不足的貨物

9. **shut-out cargo, left-off cargo, shortshipped cargo** 退關貨物

10. **overcarry** 運往他處（ *carry too far* ）

11. **shortship , leave off , shut out** 退關

12. **despatch** 〔dɪ'spætʃ〕 *v. or n.* 發送；速辦（＝ *dispatch* ）

13. **shipment** 和 **order shipment** 意思不同，前者是「裝運」後者是
「裝運貨物」。裝送貨物時可用複數的 shipments 。

order 有「訂單」「訂貨」「訂購」三種意思。

「第～號訂單」＝ order No. ～ 。訂單也可以稱爲 order sheet。
所以像以下二例這樣的句子需要格外小心。

a)　the shipment of our order　我方訂貨的裝運

b)　a shipment of our order　我方訂購的貨物（ of ＝ belong-
　　ing to ）

也就是說 a) 中的 order 是「訂貨」，shipment 是「裝運」，而
b) 中的 order 是「訂購」，a shipment 是「貨物」。再看看下
面的句子：

a)　*A* shipment of 50 packages of orange *on* our order has
　　just arrived.

　　我方訂購的五十箱柳丁的貨物，剛剛送達。（ shipment ＝
　　貨物，of 表同位格）

b)　*The* shipment *of* your order — 50 packages of orange —
　　was delayed due to the Chinese New Year.

　　貴方訂購的貨物—五十箱柳丁，因爲春節而延誤。

c)　*Your* shipment of 50 packages of orange *on* our order
　　has just arrived.

　　對於我方訂購的五十箱柳丁，貴方的貨物已經到達。

d)　*Your* shipment *of* our order for 50 packages of orange
　　has just arrived.

　　和 c) 譯法一致。

14. **a few days of grace**
　　給予幾天寬限

15. **tracer**〔'tresɚ〕*n.* 追查狀

We sent out tracers to the quarters concerned.

我方將貨物追查狀寄給有關方面。

16. **ETD** 預定開航日期（*estimated time of departure*）

ETA 預定抵埠日期（*estimated time of arrival*）

a) Your May 6 order — 100 b/s of silk products — has been loaded on s.s. "President" **ETD** Keelung on June 10.

貴方於5月6日所訂的一百綑絲織品，已裝載於總統號輪，預定於6月10日由基隆開航。

b) Your May 6 order — 100 b/s of silk products — will be loaded on s.s. "President" **ETA** Keelung on June 10.

貴方於5月6日所訂的一百綑絲織品，將裝載於總統號輪，預定於6月10日抵達基隆。

17. a) **shipped quality terms** 裝貨品質條件

b) **landed quality terms** 卸貨品質條件

c) **shipped analysis** 裝貨分析

d) **landed analysis** 卸貨分析

a）是以在裝貨時廠商的檢驗爲最終條件，b）是以在卸貨時進口商的檢驗爲最終條件。在長期的海運途中，由於暴風雨、搖晃、水氣、溫度變化或其他惡劣的條件，品質難免會起變化。因此買賣雙方必須事先協定是用 *shipped quality terms* 或 *landed quality terms*。若協議採用 shipped quality terms 的話，那麼貨品到達卸貨港口，且品質發生變化時，賣方毋須負責。若採用 landed quality terms的話，損壞責任當然由賣方負擔。c)d)也是在裝貨或卸貨港口的品質分析，必須經過協議而決定使用其中之一。無論a)b)c)d)中的任何一項，都必須透過第三者的檢驗。

18. **TEU與FEU** 兩者都是貨櫃用語，前者是 *twenty-foot equiva-lent unit* （其容積爲20′×8′×8′）後者是 *forty-foot equiva-lent unit* （其容積爲40′×8′×8′）。也就是長20呎，高8呎、寬8呎的貨櫃與長40呎、高8呎、寬8呎的大型貨櫃。一般通稱前者爲20呎標準貨櫃，後者爲40呎標準貨櫃。

Last year, Keelung Port handled some 800,000 TEUS and 200,000 FEUS.

去年基隆港共處理了八十萬個二十呎標準貨櫃，二十萬個四十呎標準貨櫃。

19. **consolidation**〔kən‚sɑlə′deʃən〕*n.* 在裝櫃時，將未滿一櫃的貨物（ *less-than-container load — LCL* ）併裝的工作。貨車、卡車也有這種情況，通稱爲合裝作業。

consolidator〔kən′sɑlə‚detɚ〕*n.* 合裝業者

20. **clean, shipped on board B/L** （參照模範書信B−1）無瑕疵已裝船提單，通稱爲**清潔提單**。

a) 貨物裝船時，必須會合貨主方面與船公司方面的點數員（tal-lyman），一同檢查貨品有否破損、浸溼或其他故障，若有瑕疵必須記載於M/R上，以後再轉載於提單上。這種有備註（remark）的貨物B/L是foul B/L（不清潔提單），銀行可以拒絕押滙。爲了能夠使銀行押滙，務必將foul改成clean才行。無remark的清潔提單稱爲clean B/L。

b) **shipped on B/L**或**shipped B/L** **裝運提單**；由於提單通常都是在貨物裝船之後才簽發的，因而命名爲shipped B/L，B/L的起頭都寫有shipped, in apparent good order and con-dition ___ the goods ___的字樣。這與在碼頭將貨物交給船公司時，簽發的**備運提單**（Received B/L）是相對的。

21. 裝運貨物的包裝及箱子都要**刷嘜**（ shipping marks ），一看到這個嘜頭就能**辨**明製造國、目的地、訂單編號及其他，顯示貨物的身份（ identity ）和目的地（ destination ）。以下是 shipping mark 的一個例子。

TK－2500
C＃5/40
NEW YORK
MADE IN TAIWAN

〈ABK〉是 main mark ，其中有代表收貨人的標幟，很容易與其他貨物辨識。以下還標示有訂單號碼、箱號、目的地與製造國，這是顯示裝運貨物的 identity，也是最重要的部分；就右圖而言，TK－2500 是訂單號碼，C＃5/40 是表示四十箱當中的第五箱，開往 NEW YORK, 台灣製造。

22. 中文的抽象名詞無論如何都是抽象名詞，但是英文中的抽象名詞只要加上不定冠詞 a ，或複數的 s ，就能轉變成普通名詞。這種法則同樣可以應用於商業英文之中，以下列舉數例，以茲參考。

抽象名詞	轉　換　成　普　通　名　詞
order （訂單）	your *order* No. 150　貴方第 150 號訂單的貨品 your *orders* Nos. 150 & 300 　　貴方第 150 及 300 號訂單的貨品
shipment （裝運）	a *shipment*　一次裝運的貨品 *shipments*　多次裝運的貨品 Your October *shipment* has not arrived to date.　貴方 10 月的運貨至今尚未到達。

	Your October and November *shipments* have not reached us to date. 貴方10月與11月的運貨至今尚未送達。
payment （支付）	a *payment*　一次的支付額 *payments* 多次的支付額 We have not yet received your *payment* for October. 　本公司尚未收到貴方10月的支付金。 His *payments* have been very irregular for some time past. 　過去有些時候他的付款很不規則。
account （帳款）	an *account*　帳款 *accounts* 帳款（複數） I am not in a position to meet this little *account* at this moment. 　我現在無法支付這筆小帳。 We have settled *accounts* with them. 　我們已與他們結清帳款。
sum （金額）	a *sum* 金額 *sums* 金額（複數） We have received a *sum* of $2,000. 　本公司收到2000元的金額。 We have received occasional *sums* of money. 　本公司偶爾收到金額。

	【說明】但是，sums 也表示金額觀念的強調。 〔例〕 huge *sums* of money（大量的金額） a huge *sum* of money（同上）
arrival （到達）	an *arrival* 到達貨品（人）（單數） *arrivals* 到達貨品（人）（複數） the first *arrivals* 最初到達的貨品 new *arrivals* 新到貨品 We checked the *arrivals* against the invoice. 本公司依發票查核到貨。
delivery （交貨）	a *delivery* 一次交貨的物品 *deliveries* 多次交貨的物品 The checking of your *delivery* proved 3 packages short of the invoiced volume. 檢查貴方的交貨，顯示比發票數量短少三箱。
return （退還）	*returns* 退貨（*returned* goods）（通常用複數） The warehouse is packed with *returns* of mill goods. 倉庫中積滿了工廠的退貨。
supply （供給）	*supplies* 補給品（通常用複數） We have placed a sizable order for manufacturing *supplies*. 本公司已訂購相當多的生產補給。

demand （需求）	a *demand* 需求項目（單數） *demands* 需求項目（複數） We have many *demands* on your last delivery. 本公司對貴方前次的交貨甚為不滿。

【說明】抽象名詞可依原樣作集合名詞如a），或是加上 s 單單作為觀念的強調，如b）。

    a） *beauty* = beautiful persons 美人

         age = aged persons 老人

         youth = young people 年輕人

    b） strong *demands* 強烈的需求

         unshakable *fears* 強烈的恐懼

         ardent *hopes* 熱切的希望

23. 承辦海運業務方面，可分以下三種：

    a）乙種海運代理業：海運代理人必須代替貿易商辦理進出口實務，諸如卸貨、點數、測重、結關手續、辦理文件等等。

    b）甲種海運代理業：是在貨物運輸需要包船時，提供船舶的 ship broker（船舶經紀人）。我國現多由船公司代理，國外則盛行由甲種海運代理人承辦，稱為 ship broker, 或 ship charter。

    c）船公司代理店 steamship agent；shipping agent

裝 運 模 範 書 信

A. 裝運指示（ Shipping Instructions ）

1

This is to confirm our May 1 telex message *running* that your order No. 56 —— 100 b/s of cotton products —— was shipped by s.s. "President" which left Keelung on the following day, for your destination. We enclose copies of B/L, invoice and Insurance policy. *To cover this shipment*, we have *drawn* on you *at sight* for the amount of the enclosed Invoice, $5,000, *through* Bank of Taiwan, Taipei. We hope you would *protect* the draft upon presentation. We trust that the shipment will be found *in order* upon arrival and will meet with your approval.

此乃確認本公司5月1日電傳，電文寫著，您第56號訂單的一百綑棉製品，裝載於次日駛離基隆的總統號輪，前往貴地。隨函奉寄提單、發票與保險單副本。我方已經由台北的台灣銀行，開給貴方與附寄的發票等值的五千元即期匯票，以便收回船貨費用。盼您在提示時承兌本匯票。相信貨品將安然抵達，並令貴方滿意。

2

A consignment of 10 Sewing Machines *on* your order has been *loaded on* the C/S "Universe" sailing from Kaohsiung Container Terminal on March 11 for your destination. Copies of B/L, Invoice and Insurance policy will be sent to you *by separate mail*. We trust the shipment will reach you safely and *in good condition*.

　　貴方訂購的十台託售縫衣機已載於宇宙號貨櫃船，將於３月11日由高雄貨櫃碼頭駛往貴地。提單、發票與保險單副本將另函奉寄。相信貨品將安然無損抵達。

3

We thank you for your letter of December 5, also for the *sailing card* enclosed and the *shipping instructions* form. We note that your M/V "Bolivia" is receiving cargo for Malta on the 10th of this month, and we will arrange for the CYCLES to *be delivered at* the West India Docks, London. Your shipping instructions form, duly completed, is enclosed.

感謝貴方 12月5日來函，及附寄的開航通知單與裝運指示表。我方注意到貴方的玻利維亞號柴油船，將於本月10日載貨前往馬爾他，我方將安排自行車於倫敦的西印度碼頭交貨。隨函奉寄適時填妥的裝運指示表。

B. 裝運通知（ **Shipping Advice** ）

1

We are pleased to inform you that the **CYCLES** have now been despatched *as arranged*:

Packing: in 30 cases 1 Cycle to One case

Marking & Numbering: **FBC** *in square* **MALTA**, 1—30 incl. Particulars of weight & measurements are given on the enclosed sheet.

Shipment: by M/V "Bolivia", ～Line, which sailed from West India Docks, London, on December 16, scheduled to arrive at Malta on December 24.

Clean, shipped on board Bs/L in complete set, together with Commercial Invoice and Insurance Certificate, both *in triplicate*, have been handed to Barkleys Bank,——with *sight draft* for £2,250,

> in accordance with the terms of the
> Letter of Credit opened *with them*. This
> sum has duly been paid by Barkleys Bank.
> We shall be pleased to hear in due course
> that the consignment has arrived safely
> and in good condition.

本公司樂於通知貴方，自行車已照約定發送如下：

包裝：分 30 箱　　每箱裝自行車一台

嘜頭及編號：

FBC　No.1 —— No.30

詳細的重量與材積列於附表。

MALTA

裝運：由～航運公司的玻利維亞號柴油船承運，該船於 12 月 16 日駛離倫敦的西印度碼頭，預定於 12 月 24 日抵達馬爾他。整套的清潔已裝船提單，與一式三份的商業發票與保險證明書，都已交給百利銀行；並依他們所開信用狀的條件，開出二千二百五十英鎊的即期滙票，此數額已由百利銀行如期支付。

若蒙適時告知此批託售貨物安然無損抵達，則感幸甚。

➡ measurement〔'mɛʒəmənt〕*n*. 材積；測得之體積

➡ triplicate〔'trɪpləkɪt〕*n*. 一式三份的文件

2

The goods of your order have now *been shipped on* the s.s. "Eastern Star" sailing tomorrow from the Port of London to Sydney. We are waiting for the Bs/L from the shipowners, and their copies will *be airmailed to* you with those of the Invoice and Insurance certificate, *in accordance with* our usual procedure.

貴方訂貨現已裝載於東方之星上，定於明日由倫敦港駛往雪梨。本公司現正等待船主開出提單，提單連同發票與保險證明的副本，將依照慣例，一併以航空郵寄給貴方。

C. 貨櫃運輸 (Container Transport)

1

Many thanks for your order No. 1234. As you *are desirous of* prompt shipment, we have immediately *got in touch with* consolidators on the matter. Fortunately, we have been able to *book the needed space* on C/S "Universe" sailing from Kaohsiung Container Terminal on January 15. Upon opening the L/C covering the same order, please wire us its number by telex.

承收貴方第1234號訂單，不勝感激。由於您盼望即期裝運，我方立刻就此事與合裝業者接洽。所幸，我方得以在將於1月15日由高雄貨櫃碼頭開航的宇宙號貨櫃船上，洽訂所需船位。一俟此訂單的信用狀開出，敬請以電傳告知我方編號。

第7章
租船契約
Charter Party; C/P

　　租下船艙的全部或一部分，將大量貨物經由海上運輸出貨。這時貨主可直接或透過 shipbroker（船務代理）和船公司締結契約，稱為租船契約。與租用火車車廂運送一樣，不同的只是海上、陸上的差別罷了。聯合運輸（combined transport—參考貨櫃運輸）時，雙方都適用的 B/L 稱為 **through B/L（聯運提單）**。租船契約中，貨主定期包下船舶的情況稱為 **time charter（定期租船）**，適用於大宗貨物往返於 A、B 兩港的情況下。相反地，只有運輸期間才租借的有 **voyage charter** 及 **trip charter（航程租船）**。一般貿易都是利用 trip charter。

　　租船契約是雇用不定期船（tamper）運送大量的 bulk cargo（散裝貨物——穀物、礦物、油類、木材等）。訂下租船契約後，船公司會簽發租船契約提單（charter party bill of lading）給發貨人。B/L 上面記有 as per charter party，信用狀也需載明由 **C/P 運輸**的字樣。租船契約主要內容有裝載貨品名稱、數量、裝船港、卸貨港、運費及付

款條件、停泊期間及開始停泊期、裝卸條件、船伕費負擔條件、滯期費、速遣費、船舶返回裝貨港日期、解約和損害賠償條件等。其中，停泊期間和開始停泊期（laytime and time commence），裝卸條件（loading and unloading terms, C.Q.D., weather working days, etc）、船伕費負擔條件（berth terms, F.I.O., F.I., F.O. terms）、滯期費（demurrage）、速遣費（despatch money）等請參考租船契約須知。

　　所謂**開始停泊期**（**laytime commence**）和裝卸貨同時，即送達船上簽發的「備裝通知」，經過規定的休息期間（respite）後開始的。在此之前是 free time，不算在 laytime 之內。卸貨作業當然是在租船到達規定的 berth（停泊處）之後開始的，但是在**港外船**（**vessel in stream**）的情況下，有時得先在港外卸貨，然後送往碼頭再卸。這時 laytime 的計算是先將港外卸貨部分與碼頭卸貨部分分開計算，然後再合併成 laytime。在港外裝運稱作「**港外裝貨**」（**off - shore loading ; loading in stream**），在港外卸貨稱為「**港外卸貨**」（**off - shore discharge ; discharge in stream**）。這兒的港外是指港內碼頭之外的泊船地點，通常設有浮標（buoy），需要極大的面積與設備。不是 open sea，而是與「停靠碼頭」相對的名詞。

租 船 契 約 必 備 例 句

A. 租船（Charter）

1. It is stipulated in the charter party that the vessel is to *proceed to a port of call*.

   租船契約上規定，本船直接開往停靠港。

   ➡ a port of call 停靠港

2. The vessel must arrive at the port of loading on or before April 10, otherwise they have the *option* of cancelling the charter.

   ➡ option〔ˊɑpʃən〕 *n.* 選擇權

船隻必須於4月10日或之前到達裝貨港，否則他們有權取消租船契約。

3. The *port-charges* must be borne on your part, as is indicated in the copy of the charter party enclosed.

如附寄的租船契約副本所指示的，港口費用必須由貴方負擔。

4. Under this charter, the vessel must call at Keelung *for orders*.

租船契約規定，船隻必須停靠基隆港裝載訂貨。

5. The ship was not to be chartered at a lower rate; you will, however, perceive that we have *procured* 30 *working days* for loading and unloading.

船隻不以較低價出租；不論如何貴方須了解我方已經得到三十個工作天裝運和卸貨。

6. We shall be glad to know if you can *fix us* a time charter for a suitable vessel.

若蒙安排給本公司一艘適宜的船隻，做為定期租船，並告知我方，則深感幸甚。

7. It would *prove most conducive to* your interest to charter a vessel in your port.

在貴港包租一艘船對貴方非常有利。

8. The charterers have to find a sufficient number of small packages for *broken stowage*.

租船者對零碎的裝載量必須找小包裹補足。

9. The shipowner guarantees to the charterers and consignors the *seaworthiness* of the vessel during the voyage.

船主對租船者和委託人保證該船在航行期間的適航性。

　➡ consignor〔kən'saɪnɚ〕 *n.* 委託人

10. Charterers are of the opinion that shipowners are responsible for leakage *as per C/P Clause* 9.

租船者的看法是，依照租船契約第九條船主對漏損負責。

　➡ leakage〔'likɪdʒ〕 *n.* 漏損

11. If the vessel is not ready to load by a stated date, called the *cancelling date*, charterers have the option of cancelling the charter.

若本船不能在指定日期——稱爲取消日期，準備載貨，租船者有權取消租船契約。

B. 停泊和裝卸條件（Laytime & Stevedoring Terms）

1. There is no steamer *on the berth* for San Francisco at present.

目前在停泊處沒有開往舊金山的船。

2. What are the prospects for loading on the berth?

對在停泊處裝貨的希望如何？

3. They cannot **berth** the vessel **alongside the pier**.

　　➡ pier〔pɪr〕*n*. 碼頭；防波堤

他們不能在防波堤橫靠本船。

4. The vessel **is in berth** and is loading and unloading.

本船到達停泊港，正在裝卸貨物。

5. The counting of **laytime** is not always subject to the vessel **arriving on the berth**.

停泊期的計算不一定以船到達停泊港為條件。

6. The charter party provides that Sundays and Holidays are excepted, even if used, in the counting of laydays.

租船契約規定，星期例假日即使被使用，也不算在停泊期限內。

7. The charter party provides that Sundays and Holidays are excepted, unless used, in the counting of laydays.

租船契約規定，星期例假日除非被使用，否則不算在停泊期限內。

8. Cargo to be discharged at the average rate of not less than 1,000 tons per **weather working day**, **SHEX**, and if longer detained, the receivers are to pay the owners **demurrage** at the rate of $1,500 US Currency per day or **pro rata** for part of a day.

星期例假日除外，晴天工作日卸貨平均不得少於一千噸，若延誤過久，收貨人須按每天美金通貨一千五百元，若不滿一天則按比例付滯期費給船主。

9. Owners shall pay the Charterers ***despatch money*** at the rate of $500 US Currency per day or ***pro rata*** for part of a day for all laytime saved in loading and discharging.

 ➡ despatch money 速遣費

船主對裝卸貨物省下的停泊時間，按照每天美金通貨五百元，或者不滿一天時，按照比率付給租船者速遣費。

10. Vessels to be loaded at the average rate of not less than 200,000 ***bd.ft***. per ***W.W.D.***, ***SHEX unless used***.

除非使用，星期例假日除外，每個晴天工作日，船隻裝貨平均比率不少於二十萬材積。

11. ***Customary Quick Despatch or***, ***C.Q.D***. generally applies to the laytime of a regular liner, sometimes, of a chartered vessel.

C.Q.D. —— 習慣快速裝卸——普通適用於定期輪船的停泊期，有時候也適用於租船。

12. Detention by quarantine not to be reckoned as laydays.

隔離檢疫的耽擱不算在停泊期內。

13. ***Berth terms*** generally applies to a regular liner on the condition of C.Q.D., while ***F.I.O***., ***F.I.***, ***or F.O***. applies to a ***tramper*** which a shipper charters for the transport of his ***bulk cargo***.

停泊條款通常適用於 C.Q.D. 情況的定期輪船，而 F.I.O.、F.I. 或 F.O. 適用於貨主為了運送散裝貨物所租的不定期貨船。（* F.I.Q.、F.I.、F.O. 請詳見租船契約須知）

14. Under the **berth terms**, loading and unloading charges are for the account of the shipowner, while the **F.I.O.**, **F.I.** or **F.O.** **terms** relieve the owner from these expenses totally or partly which are to be borne by the charterer.

依停泊條款，裝卸費用由船主負擔，而在 F.I.O.、F.I.或F.O.的條款下，使船主免除全部或部分裝卸費用，而由租船者負擔。

15. The owner of a tramper does not **collect cargo**, but does lease his ship to a consignor or other owner by which to produce his revenue.

不定期貨船的船主不收集貨物，但是將船出租給委託人或其它船主，以產生收益。

16. The laytime in loading and discharge is generally to commence at 7 or 8 a.m. on **the first working day**, SHEX, after the delivery of the **Notice of Readiness**.

➡ Notice of Readiness 備裝通知

裝卸貨物的停泊期通常從備裝通知送達後，第一個工作天早上七或八點開始，星期例假日除外。

17. Out of the total cargo of 5,000 tons, 2,000 tons were loaded **in stream** and the remainder at wharf, both on **W.W.D. terms**.

➡ **to load in stream** 港外裝貨

總貨物量在五千噸到二千噸則在港外裝貨，剩餘的在碼頭裝貨，兩者皆以晴天工作日為條件。

18. C/P clause stipulates loading 400 tons *in stream* and 500 tons at wharf per W.W. Day. Loading in stream needs 5 days and that at wharf 6 days, resulting in the total *laytime allowed* being 11 days. However, the vessel spent one day and a half, shifting its position from stream to wharf and waiting for the arrival of part of the cargo. Thus the actual *laytime used* was 12 days and a half with the charterer's obligation of paying a demurrage for 1.5 days.

租船契約規定，晴天工作日在港外裝貨四百噸，在碼頭裝貨五百噸。在港外裝貨需時五天，在碼頭裝貨需時六天，規定的停泊期總共十一天。但是，船隻從港外移到碼頭，並等待部分貨物，費時一天半。因此實際使用的停泊期是十二天半，租船者須負擔一天半的滯期費。

19. Despatch money is a kind of remuneration to be paid to the charterer by the owner for *all laytime saved* in loading and unloading at port. The sum of the despatch money, however, is normally the half of the demurrage rate to be paid by the charterer to the owner for the time used beyond the laytime allowed.

速遣費是船主將在港口裝卸貨物所節省下來的停泊期，支付給租船者的報酬。然而速遣費的總額通常是在超過允許的停泊期間，租船者付給船主滯期費的一半。

➡ remuneration〔rɪ,mjunə'reʃən〕*n.* 報酬

20. **"*Gang*"** is a unit of longshoremen engaged in loading and unloading at port. One gang usually consists of 10 to 12 members.

「班」是碼頭工人在港口從事裝貨和卸貨的單位。一班通常包括十到十二個成員。

➡ longshoreman 〔'lɔŋ͵ʃɔrmən〕 *n*. 碼頭工人

21. Immediate gang arrangement is necessary in preparation for the vessel's arrival in port tomorrow.

有必要立刻安排裝卸作業，以備明天本船進港。

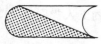 租　船　契　約　須　知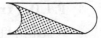

1. **laydays** (*or* **laytime**) 停泊期。租船契約用語，是指船舶進港起到裝卸結束爲止的時間。

2. **working days** 工作日。是船舶停靠期間，除去星期例假日，包括惡劣天氣的日數，二十四小時作業（working day of 24 consecutive hours）的裝卸貨天數。

3. **weather working days（W.W.D）** 最常用於從 working days 扣除惡劣天氣天數後的日數，稱爲「晴天工作日」，天氣好時二十四小時作業（Weather working day of 24 consecutive hours）。

4. **running days** 傭船契約上所訂的，在卸貨港作業，無論星期假日及天氣惡劣，二十四小時連續工作，一直到完成卸貨時的總天數，稱爲「連續工作日」。

5. **Customary Quick Despatch**（**C.Q.D.**）此爲租船在港口儘速完成裝卸作業的習慣，沒有限定每天的卸貨數量。通常這種C.Q.D. system 適用於定期船，稱爲「習慣快速裝卸」，通常直接稱爲C.Q.D.

6. **berth** 船舶在港內停留的位置。船舶必須停靠在港長（port master）按船的噸位及載重量所指定的位置。防波堤（pier）、碼頭（wharf）、突堤（quay）及港內有浮標（buoy）畫分的區域就是 berth。

   The vessel is on the berth alongside the pier.
   船舶橫靠在防波堤旁邊。

7. **berth terms**（*or*, **liner terms**）停泊條款。租船契約規定船內工人費（裝卸工人—— stevedores ——的裝卸費）和卸貨費都由船主負擔。

8. **F.I.O.**（**free in and out**）租船契約中規定，船內工人費與卸貨費都由租船人負擔。

9. **F.I.**（**free in**）租船契約中規定，由租船人負責裝貨費，由船主負責卸貨費。

10. **F.O.**（**free out**）同上，契約規定由租船人負責卸貨，由船主負責裝貨。

    ** in ＝裝貨　out ＝卸貨　free 是船主無責任

11. **Notice of Readiness**（**N/R**）備裝通知，就是完成裝卸及檢疫之後，由租船向 shipper 或 receiver 發出的通知。停泊期間（laytime）就是在發送N/R之後，經過規定的休息時間，開始計算的。

12. **SHEX** 即「**Sundays and Holidays Excepted**」的縮寫，是星期、例假日除外之意。

13. **SHEX if used** 星期例假日即使被使用也不算在停泊期限內。

14. **SHEX unless used** 星期例假日除非被使用，否則不算在停泊期限內，意即如果用星期例假日裝運，則須算入 laydays 之內。

15. **demurrage**〔dɪˈmɝdʒ〕*n*. 滯期費。租船契約規定，船舶因裝卸作業而超出規定的停泊期間（laytime allowed）時，租船人必須按比率（依時間計），每日支付船主額外的費用。稱爲demurrage。星期例假日亦徵收。

16. **despatch money** 速遣費。租船契約規定，當裝卸作業於允許停泊期限前完成，則船主要按比率（依時間計算）每日扣還租船人些許費用，通常是泊船費的一半。稱爲速遣費——可以早點啓航之意。是對所節約的允許停泊期間的付款。

17. **pro rata** 按比率計算（according to the rate, in proportion, proportionately）
    Wages are paid pro rata for his working days.
    工資按照他的工作時間支付。

18. **in stream** 在海上（港內有buoy的泊船處——berth）（參考本章開頭說明部分）

19. **laytime allowed** 允許停泊期間

20. **bd.ft.** *board foot* 的縮寫。容積單位，也稱爲Board Measure（BM），1材積＝1″×1′×1′，表厚度一英吋的木材一平方英呎的面積。

21. **gang** 指港灣勞務作業時的班或組，以四班、五班工作時，稱爲4 gangs, 5 gangs，1 gang約由十人到十二人構成。

22. **gang arrangement** 安排裝卸作業

23. **clause 9 of C/P** 租船契約書中，依其運輸品而分成許多不同契約。現在讓我們來看看以略號GENCON（General Contract）爲名，而著稱的Baltic and White Sea Conference Uniform General Charter，有關其損害賠償的clause 9。

Owners are to be responsible for loss of or damage to the goods or for delay in delivery of the goods only in case the loss, damage or delay has been caused by the improper or negligent stowage of the goods (unless stowage performed by shippers or their stevedores or servants) or by personal want of due diligence on the part of the Owners or their Manager to make the vessel in all respects seaworthy and to secure that she is properly manned, equipped and supplied or by the personal act or default of the Owners or their Manager.

And the Owners are responsible for no loss or damage or delay arising from any other cause whatsoever, even from the neglect or default of the captain or crew or some other person employed by the Owners on board or ashore for whose acts they would, but for this clause, be responsible, or from unseaworthiness of the vessel on loading or commencement of the voyage or at any time whatsoever.

Damage caused by contact with or leakage, smell or evaporation from other goods or by the inflammable or explosive nature or insufficient package of other goods not to be considered as caused by improper or negligent stowage, even if in fact so caused.

〔主旨〕A. 船主只對以下情況所發生的貨物遺失、受損、延遲交貨，負有責任。

　　1. 由不適當或裝載不小心所引起的貨物遺失、受損、延遲交貨時，但由發貨人或其裝卸工人裝運時引起的則不算在內。

2. 從所有觀點來看，船主或船舶管理者個人未保持船舶適航性上，採取適當的人員分配、適當的設備供給的措施而引起時。

3. 這類事故起因於船主、船舶管理員個人行為或個人的怠慢。

B. 船主對以下列舉的原因所導致的貨物遺失、受損、延遲交貨，概不負責：即使船長、船員或船中、陸上雇請備工所必須負責的行為，引起的怠慢、不履行契約、抑或是在裝貨、航海開始及其他時候，因船舶缺乏適航性而引起時，不必負責。

C. 由於接觸其他物品，或藉由其他物品產生漏損、臭氣傳播、水分發散、易燃性、爆炸物質、包裝不完善而引起的損害，不能視為因不適當或不小心裝運所引起的損害。

24. **stowage** 裝載。是指船中裝卸工人裝運貨物。

25. **broken stowage** → stowage of cargo with vacant spaces left in it（Webster 3rd edition），貨物艙尚留有空間的裝載。這種多餘空際就稱為 brokcn space，要用較小的貨物將此空際填補起來（參考租船必備例句中A「租船」的例題8）。

26. **bulk cargo** 散裝貨物。未加以包裝而運送的貨物。租船契約中交易物為大宗穀物、木材、油類、礦物時，稱為 bulk cargo。

租 船 契 約 模 範 書 信

A. 租船（Charter）

1

We are due to ship a large quantity of sugar to
Montreal and should be glad if you would *procure*

us a steamer with a cargo capacity of approximately 1,500 tons. Owing to the fact that the cargo is to be delivered by August 15, the vessel we have in mind is one capable of *maintaining a steady ten knots*. As the transaction in question leaves but a small margin of profit, the question of fuel consumption demands careful consideration. The vessel will be required to proceed to Newcastle for loading and we trust that you will make every effort to reduce our expenses by *chartering* a ship now in northern waters. An early estimate of the expenses involved would enable us to give you definite instructions without delay.

我們預定以船運大量的糖到蒙特婁，若蒙爲本公司取得一艘容貨量大約一千五百噸的輪船，則感幸甚。由於必須在 8 月 15 日前交貨，我方想要的是一艘能夠維持十海里穩定速度的船。因爲所談的交易只有微薄的利潤，燃料的耗損需要愼重的考慮。船隻必須前往紐加塞港裝貨，相信貴方會盡全力租一艘現在北方水域的船，以減低我方的費用。早日估量有關費用將使我方能夠立即給貴方明確的指示而不致延誤。

➡ knot〔nɑt〕*n*. 海里；浬（記船之時速的單位）
➡ transaction〔træns'ækʃən〕*n*. 交易

2

We have entered into a contract for the supply of Motor Vehicles and Parts, over the next six months, to West Africa and shall be glad to know if you can *fix us a time charter for a suitable vessel.* The question of *speed* must be considered as the ship should be able to *make* 3 *voyages* in the time, allowing ten days for loading and unloading on each voyage. In view of the *general slackness* of the market at the moment, we hope that you can get us a really good offer.

本公司締結一項下六個月供應西非汽車和零件的契約，如蒙告知可以爲我方安排一艘適當的船做爲定期租船，則感幸甚。速度問題要加以考慮，因爲在那段時間必須做三次航行，而每次航行須酌留十天以裝卸貨物。鑑於此時市場普遍蕭條，本公司希望貴方能爲我方找到實在合理的報價。

3

In confirmation of our telex to you today, a copy of which we enclose, we are pleased to say we have found what we think should be a very suitable vessel for your purpose : the M/V MERCURY, cargo capacity ～

> tons, average speed ～ knots. She is, perhaps, a
> little larger than you require but the owners are
> prepared to consider a special rate for a time
> charter. We hope this fixture will suit you and as
> soon as we receive your confirmation we will prepare
> the Charter Party.

確認本公司今天發給貴方的電傳，茲附上電文副本，我方很樂意說明，我方已經找到一艘認為非常適合您的目的的船隻：馬克里號輪，容貨量～噸，平均速度～海里。或許比貴方要求的稍微大些，但是船主準備為定期租船考慮給予特價優待。本公司希望這次定期租船能適合您，一俟接到貴方的確認書，就會準備租船契約。

B. 備裝通知（Notice of Readiness）

以下所示者是為Notice of Readiness（備裝通知）的形式，畫線部分要填入或簽署。

1

> This is to advise you that the above vessel arrived
> at [*Port*] at [*Time*] hours on [*Date*] and she is in
> all respects ready to commence discharge/loading
> in accordance with the terms and conditions of the
> Charter Party.
> Notice tendered at [*Time*] hours on [*Date*].

Signed

Master s.s. 〔*Vessel Name*〕

Notice accepted at 〔*Time*〕 hours on 〔*Date*〕.

For Charterer

　　　　〔*company name*〕

　　　Signed

　　　　Manager

　　本文是通知貴方上述船隻在～日～時到達～港口，並且完全準備開始依據租船契約的條款和條件卸貨／裝貨。

　　　　通知書在～日～時提出

　　　　～船船長　簽名

　　　　通知書在～日～時　收到

　　　　　租船者

　　　　　　〔公司名稱〕

　　　　　　經理　簽名

【說明】　Notice of Readiness 的形式如上，將這一張 print 分　　　別送交發貨人、收貨人，簽章以示確認領貨。

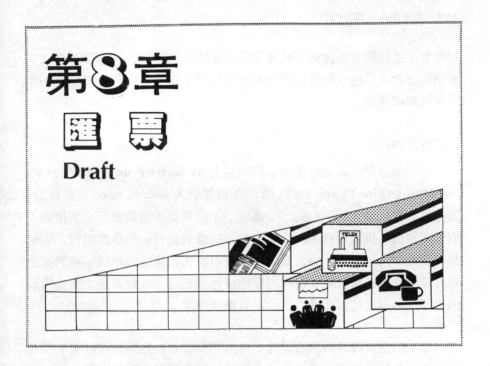

第8章
匯 票
Draft

1.信用狀付款　Settlement by L/C

　　依據第五章信用狀所述，通常信用狀是依開狀銀行→通知銀行→出口商的順序傳遞，出口商在領到信用狀後就準備裝運事宜。完成裝船之後，持承做的**裝運文件（shipping documents）**併信用狀正本至銀行，開出一張以**信用狀上載明之抬頭人（外滙銀行或進口商）**爲付款人的滙票，至於是即期或遠期滙票，則需視信用狀的規定。爲避免滙票遺失，應該開出正副兩張，各附上裝運文件的正副本，以不同的信封郵寄給抬頭銀行或開狀銀行。

　　出口商開出的滙票，通常是由通知銀行購票，因爲通知銀行經常身兼押滙銀行（negotiating bank）。押滙之後，信用狀正本就由押滙銀

行保管，並將購入的滙票和裝運文件寄給進口地銀行,請求付款或承兌。滙票的付款人爲進口商時，應把滙票寄給開狀銀行，由其提出給進口商,請求付款或承兌。

● 滙票的抬頭人

滙票的抬頭人就是付款人，信用狀上 **we hereby authorize you to draw (value) upon** 〔　〕,的〔　〕塡付款人（ on 或 upon 之後接的就是滙票的抬頭人，即付款人）。通常，不論即期或遠期滙票，其抬頭人有 1.進口商 2.開狀銀行 3.開狀銀行指定的倫敦或紐約的外滙銀行。以外幣付款時，爲了金融上的方便，通常都以第 3.爲滙票的抬頭，這個指定銀行是開狀銀行在倫敦、紐約的分行或往來銀行。也就是說，做爲抬頭的銀行，必須位於以此貨幣爲法定貨幣的國家。

以 1.的進口商爲抬頭的情況，目前不多。2.自然用於非外幣，而是以台幣付款的時候，抬頭人是以台幣爲法定貨幣在台灣的銀行。

● 進口費用的支付──外幣

1. 即期滙票，抬頭爲進口商時（少）：

押滙銀行將滙票和裝運文件寄往進口地的開狀銀行，銀行再向進口商提出滙票，付款之後，再交付裝運文件。

2. 遠期滙票，抬頭爲進口商時（少）：

開狀銀行將押滙銀行寄來的遠期滙票向進口商提出，請求承兌，承兌之後再交付裝運文件。

3. 即期滙票，抬頭爲開狀銀行指定的倫敦或紐約之外滙銀行時（多）：

抬頭銀行支付押滙銀行寄來的滙票（裝運文件乃正副兩張分別與滙票第一張和第二張，以不同的郵件寄達抬頭銀行的），把裝運文件和付款通知書寄給開狀銀行。開狀銀行再向進口商提出付款通知書，

請求支付以交換裝運文件。

4. 遠期滙票，抬頭爲倫敦或紐約的外滙銀行時（多）：

押滙銀行把滙票及裝運文件寄給抬頭銀行。抬頭銀行立即承兌滙票，向當地開狀銀行寄送承兌通知。開狀銀行基於此承兌通知，向進口商開出一張等金額，但支付日期早一天的滙票，請求承兌以換取裝運文件。

● **進口費用的支付──台幣**

1. 即期滙票，抬頭爲開狀銀行時：

押滙銀行將滙票及裝運文件交給開狀銀行，銀行立即付款，然後請求進口商支付，以交換裝運文件。若進口商沒有支付資金，就先以信託收據（ Trust Receipt ）交換裝運文件。

2. 遠期滙票，抬頭爲開狀銀行時：

押滙銀行寄來裝運文件和滙票，開狀銀行於承兌時，同時開出一張等金額早一天付款的滙票給進口商，請求承兌以交換裝運文件。

2.**D/P·D/A滙票付款** Settlement by D/P or D/A Draft

貿易、外滙管理自由化的今天，若要在國際間參與出口競爭，就不能堅持只以信用狀付款。L/C（信用狀）付款對進口商來說，讓保證金長期凍結，構成很大的負擔，並不是可喜的現象。中南美諸國早有不用L/C的習慣。堅持L/C原則，在國際競爭中必落於人後。因爲不需信用狀保證的**滙票付款（ D/P , D/A滙票）**方式已經問世。**D/P**是Docu-ments against Payment（ **付款後交單據** ），進口商付清出口商開出的滙票，即可領到裝運文件；**D/A**是Documents against Accept-ance（ **承兌後交單據** ），進口商承兌了由出口商開出的滙票之後，就可

拿到裝運文件的方式。

D/P和D/A都不需要L/C，所以外滙銀行不負責購票。這時外滙銀行就成了「**託收銀行（collecting bank）**」，將出口商開出的D/P、D/A滙票送達進口地銀行，受託向進口商託收（collection）出口費用或要求出口商承兌（acceptance）滙票。或者外滙銀行還是購票，但要出口商支付margin money（保證金），由銀行保管直到進口商付款爲止。

出口商在進口商款項未經銀行送抵之前，完全沒有進款，資金周轉可能有困難。但是若投保政府的出口保險，就有百分之八十的保證，再加上地方公共團體的融通資金有百分之十五的保證，共有百分之九十五的保證，就可以請求外滙銀行購票。外滙銀行購票之後，將滙票送交進口地銀行，向進口商催繳貨款。

D/A滙票付款時，進口商一經承兌滙票後，出口商就必須交出裝運文件，所以，若非進口商有相當的信用，出口商不會貿然採用這種方式。相反地，進口商承兌D/A滙票，得到裝船文件之後，就可以銷售貨品，到滙票期滿再付款，是非常方便的。

D/P、D/A滙票面上都蓋有D/P、D/A的戳記，滙票抬頭人是長期直接進口商。因此，滙票上的文字，和L/C滙票上Drawn under〔L/C開立銀行和L/C編號〕、charge the same to account of〔進口商〕的差別只是將括號〔 〕部分空白不填。因爲它是不帶L/C的滙票，以直接進口商爲抬頭之故。其餘部分完全一樣。總之，D/P、D/A滙票都不利出口商而利於進口商，這三種安全性是按L/C→D/P→D/A的順序而逐漸降低。

D/P滙票通常以卽期爲原則，但是也有遠期的情況。（參考第十一章T/R和L/G信託收據和保證書）。以D/A、D/P方式交易的國家有歐洲、中南美洲、加拿大、大洋洲及南洋群島。

滙 票 必 備 例 句

A. 開出滙票（Drawing of Draft）

1. Today we have **drawn**（**valued**）**on you for** $〔金額〕**in favor of**〔押滙銀行〕.

   今天本公司開立給貴方，以〔押滙銀行〕爲抬頭，〔金額〕的滙票。

   ➡ **in favor of** ~ 以~爲抬頭；付與

2. This is to inform you that today we have valued on you **at sight through**〔押滙銀行〕**under** the irrevocable L/C No. ~ issued by〔信用狀開狀銀行〕**covering** our order No. ~.

   今天本公司經由〔押滙銀行〕，以〔信用狀開狀銀行〕爲支付本公司第~號訂單，而發行的編號~不可撤銷信用狀爲本，開立卽期滙票給貴方，特此奉告。

3. Today we drew upon you **at**（**by**）**30 d/s** for the amount of the enclosed invoice, $〔金額〕, which you will please **protect**.

   今天本公司照附寄的發票額〔金額〕，開給貴方見票後三十天內付款的滙票，請貴方承兌。

   ➡ protect〔prəˈtɛkt〕v. 承兌；準備支付金

4. Today we drew on you at sight, *for account of* 〔進口商〕, for the full invoice value of £ 〔金額〕 *in favor of* 〔押滙銀行〕, under the irrevocable L/C No. ～ issued by 〔信用狀開狀銀行〕.

今天本公司以〔信用狀開發銀行〕發行的第～號不可撤銷信用狀爲本，按發票總額〔金額〕英鎊，付款人〔進口商〕，受益人〔押滙銀行〕的即期滙票給貴方。

➡ *for account of* ～ 以～爲付款人

5. We have attached our *sight draft on* you for $ 〔金額〕 to the shipping documents and handed them to *our bankers* for forwarding to you.

本公司已經隨同裝運文件,附上開立給貴方〔金額〕的即期滙票，並且已經交由我方交易銀行轉寄給貴方。

6. We have drawn on you for $5,000 *through* the Bank of America, which is instructed to *surrender* the Bill of Lading *against* the payment of the draft.

本公司已經由美國銀行開給貴方五千元的滙票，並指示其於滙票付款後交付提單。

➡ *Bill of Lading* 提單

7. You may *draw on* our London agents, Messrs. ～ *at (by) 60 d/s* for the amount of your invoice. Our agents have been instructed accordingly and advised of the terms of our agreement.

貴方可以您的發票總額，開給本公司倫敦代理商——～公司見票後六十天（按）付款的滙票。我方按所說的情形連絡並通知該代理商我們的協定條件。

8. Today we **valued on you** through Bank of Taiwan for $1,000 at 30 d/s. We hope our draft will **meet your kind protection**.

今天本公司經由台灣銀行，開給貴方一千元見票後三十天付款的滙票，希望貴方好意承兌。

9. We have drawn on you **for account of** Messrs. Henderson & Co. for $1,000 A/S in favor of the Taiwan Trading Co. Kindly protect the draft **upon presentation**.

我方已經開給貴方一張以韓德遜公司爲付款人、金額一千元、受益人爲台灣貿易公司的即期滙票。在滙票提出時，請予以承兌。

10. We feel it necessary to advise drastic price-cuts all round if **anything like a satisfactory trade is to be worked up**. We should appreciate, therefore, your drawing at, say, 20 per cent **off your invoice value**.

如果要建立任何令人滿意的交易，本公司認爲通知全面徹底減價是必要的。因此，若貴方開低於發票額百分之二十的滙票，將不勝感激。

➡ drastic〔'dræstɪk〕*adj.* 徹底的；猛烈的
➡ **work up** 逐漸建立

11. We have received your letter of March 1 with **advice of draft on us for** £1,000, which is duly noted, and the same will be honored on presentation.

貴方3月1日通知開給本公司一千英鎊滙票的來函，業已收到。我方會及時注意，一經提出就會如期付款。

➡ honor〔'ɑnɚ〕*v.*〔商〕如期付款；承諾兌現（滙票等）

12. Today we drew upon you through Bank of Taiwan, Taipei, **by sight D/P** (*or by* **60 d/s D/A**) for \$6,000 covering your order No. 505—100 NIKON CAMERAS Model FE—10 AT——of our shipment. Please **protect** (*or*, **accept**) the draft upon presentation by your bankers.

今天本公司經由台北的台灣銀行開給貴方六千元，見票即付付款後交單據的滙票（或見票後六十天付款，承兌後交單據），以支付我方對貴方505號訂單——FE—10 AT型尼康照相機一百台——的貨運費。若經貴方外滙銀行提出，請即付款（承兌）。

➡ D/P = *documents against payment* 付款後交單據
➡ D/A = *documents against acceptance* 承兌後交單據

B. 滙票的支付、承兌、託收

1. Your draft of March 2, **value** \$1,000, has been presented and duly **honored to your debit**, although no advice of the drawing of it had been received from you.

貴方3月2日金額一千元的滙票已經提出，且雖然未接到貴方所開的滙票通知，已經即時如期付款，記入貴方借記。

2. Your draft on Messrs. Henderson & Co., **value** \$1,000, came to hand. This has been duly honored and the proceeds **placed to the credit of your account**.

貴方開給韓德遜公司金額一千元的滙票已經接到。並即時如期付款，實收額已歸入貴方貸方的帳戶。

➡ proceeds〔prə'sidz〕*n.* 實收額

3. Your draft of March 1 has been *accepted* and will be given due protection.

貴方 3 月 1 日開出的滙票已接到，我方已準備如期承兌。

4. We are willing to accept your draft for the amount involved *payable at* 60 *days' sight*.

我方願意承兌貴方開立的見票後六十天付款滙票的總額。

5. Please *surrender* the enclosed documents to our customer on his acceptance of the attached draft on him at 60 days for $5,000.

➡ surrender〔sə'rɛndə〕v. 讓渡

在我方的客戶承兌了附寄的、開給他的見票六十天後付款，金額五千元的滙票後，請把附寄的文件交給他。

6. *Our draft for* $3,000 *on this firm, due at* 3 *months*, is enclosed, and we ask you to present this for acceptance *against surrender* of documents and to *collect* the amount *due at maturity*.

➡ maturity〔mə'tjʊrətɪ〕n. 期滿；到期

茲附上我方開給這家公司三千元、三個月到期的滙票，並要求貴方提出以得到承兌，再交出裝運文件，並於期滿日託收本金額。

7. We are sending you the enclosed draft on Messrs. Watts & Tyler, of your city, value $3,000, which *please be good enough to collect* and credit to our account.

附寄上開給貴城瓦特及泰勒公司，面額三千元的滙票，請好意代爲託收，並記入我方貸方的帳戶。

8. We trust **you will find the acceptance in order**.

   請查收承兌滙票。

9. We return your draft duly accepted and **made payable at** ～
   Bank, which we trust you will
   find in order.

   寄回貴方開立的滙票，
   已如期承兌，可於～銀
   行請款，敬請查收。

10. We have received your letter of
    July 23 enclosing your **acceptance**
    No. 90, **due** August 30, for $3,000,
    for which we feel much obliged.

    貴方7月23日寄出，編號
    90，8月30日到期的三
    千元承兌滙票已收悉，
    並不勝感激。

11. The following drafts will shortly
    be presented to you by foreign
    drawers. Please accept them on
    our behalf and **meet them at ma-
    turity** to the debit of our account.

    下列滙票短期內將由外
    國發票人提出給貴方。
    請代本公司承兌，並於
    期滿日付款，記入我方
    帳戶之借方。

    ➡ **on one's behalf** 代表某人

12. Your acceptance for $1,000
    drawn by us on March 2 and pay-
    able to our **order** 60 d/s, **fell
    due** yesterday and now **lies at**
    our bankers. We therefore re-
    quest you to **take up** the same.

    經貴方承兌的，我方3
    月2日開立的見票六十
    天後支付給我方指定銀
    行的一千元滙票，於昨
    天到期，現仍保管於我
    方銀行。因此懇請貴方
    支付此金額。

    ➡ **take up** （支票、滙票）承兌；支付

C. 拒絕支付、拒絕承兌滙票（Non-Payment & Non-Acceptance of Draft）

1. We regret to inform you that your two *acceptances* were *returned dishonored* (*rejected*) by the bank.

很遺憾通知貴方，您承兌的兩張滙票，都遭銀行退票（拒付）。

> ➡ dishonor〔dɪsˈɑnə〕v. 拒絕支付（支票、滙票）；退票

2. We are very much surprised to find that your acceptance for $1,000 *due* on March 1, *payable* Bank of Taiwan, Taipei, has been duly presented, but returned to us, *dishonored*.

發現經貴方承兌，付款地台北的台灣銀行，3月1日到期的一千元滙票，雖經即時提出，卻遭退票，我方甚爲驚訝。

3. We are sorry to hear of the *nonacceptance* of our draft.

得知我方的滙票未獲承兌，深以爲憾。

4. We were surprised to receive information from our bankers this morning that your acceptance for $2,000, *due* on December 10, has been *dishonored*.

今天早上接到我方交易銀行的通知，得知經貴方承兌，12月10日到期的二千元滙票遭退票，我方深感驚訝。

5. We were shocked to learn that the *acceptance* of our draft has been *refused*.

得知我方滙票的承兌遭退票，深感震驚。

6. This morning, to our great surprise and annoyance, our bankers
returned our bill ***on*** you for
$ 1,000, due on March 10, marked
"***No Funds.***"

→ annoyance 〔ə'nɔɪəns〕 *n.* 煩惱

今天早上,我方交易銀
行將開立給貴方 3 月10
日到期的一千元滙票,
以「 無資金 」爲由退回,
使我方大爲驚訝和煩惱。

7. This being the case, we request
your immediate payment ***in cash***
and also your reply convincing
and satisfactory to us.

有鑑於此,懇請貴方立
即以現金付款,並給我
方滿意的答覆。

8. We give you notice that unless
we receive the cash（not a
cheque）by April 10, we shall
sue for the amount without
further delay.

→ sue 〔su〕 *v.* 提出訴訟;和…打官司

請貴方注意,除非我方
於 4 月10日前接到現金
（ 不是支票 ）,否則將
立即對此金額提出訴訟。

9. Our position is particularly
difficult, as ***we are burdened***
with taking up your drafts for
sums far in excess of the
funds ***we hold at your dispos-***
al.

→ ***at one's disposal*** 由～支配;隨～自由

因爲身負支付貴方滙票
的責任,而該筆金額遠
超過按您的指示我方可
以處理的現款,所以本
公司處境格外艱難。

10. To our great surprise, a bill drawn by you on us *for the goods* consigned by s.s. "Mogul" was presented today *for acceptance*. We naturally refused to take up the bill. The reason is that....

　　貴方對蒙古號輪承運的貨物，開立給本公司的滙票，我方對今日的提出承兌感到驚訝。我方自當拒付，原因是…。

11. If the draft is not immediately *taken up*, we shall be compelled to *have recourse to measures no less unpleasant to us than disagreeable to yourselves*.

　　若不立即支付本滙票，我方將不得不採取適當措施，這是對您我雙方都不愉快的事。

　➡ recourse 〔rɪ'kors〕 *n.* 求助；依賴

拒絕支付、拒絕承兌滙票的結尾語

1. We request your immediate payment of the *amount*.

　　我方要求貴方立刻付款。

2. We request your immediate reply *in this instance*.

　　懇請貴方立即答覆此事。

3. Your failure in sending the amount by〔date〕will force us to *take legal procedures*.

　　貴方如不於〔日期〕前將款項寄來，本公司將不得不採取法律途徑。

D. L/C→D/P, D/P→D/A的變更（Change from L/C to D/P, D/P to D/A）

1. Your *D/P draft for the shipment* by s.s. "Calcutta" has been presented and *duly met*. We should now like to ask you if you are willing to supply us in future *on* 60 *d/s*, *D/A terms*, as other suppliers in your country are already allowing us this credit.

貴方對加爾各答號輪裝運費所開出的付款後交單據滙票已經提出，並即期付款。現在本公司想要求貴方，今後是否願意以承兌後交單據、見票後六十天付款爲條件供應本公司，因爲貴國的其它供應商都已經給予我方這種信任。

➡ D/P = documents against payment　付款後交單據
➡ D/A = documents against acceptance　承兌後交單據

2. We regret to be unable to meet your wish for a change from L/C to D/P basis because we are now finding difficulty in *money operation* and, moreover, under the D/P system quick *money collection* is impossible nor is there any guarantee for payment.

本公司無法允諾貴方的要求，將信用狀基準改爲付款後交單據基準，因爲我方現在金錢運轉有困難，何況在付款後交單據的制度下，不可能迅速回收資金，付款也沒有保障，我方深感抱歉。

E. 遺失滙票（Missing of Draft）

1. We cabled to you today **reading**
   "FIRST OF EXCHANGE$2,000
   ON NATIONAL BANK OUR
   ORDER, MISSING" and received
   your cabled reply **reading** "DULY
   FORWARDED WITH ADVICE.
   STOP PAYMENT."

   今天拍發給貴方的電文
   爲「我方指定人國民銀
   行付款的二千元滙票之
   第一張遺失。」，並收
   到貴方「確實已將滙票
   及通知書寄上。停止付
   款。」的回覆電文。

2. We regret to inform you that
   we are unable to trace receipt
   of the First of Exchange, value $2,000 —— advised in your
   letter of March 7. Owing to **an
   irregularity in opening our letters**, we cannot say definitely
   whether this bill was enclosed
   or not.

   貴方3月7日來信通知
   的，金額二千元的第一
   張滙票收據，很抱歉本
   公司無法追查到。由於
   發信偶一不規則，故不
   能確定此滙票是否附寄
   過。

3. We have immediately informed
   the drawees of the **mishap**
   and requested them to pay
   only against the presentation of
   the Second of Exchange through
   our bankers, and with our own
   endorsement.

   我方已即時通知滙票付
   款人此次不幸事件，並
   要求只有經我方交易銀
   行提出，且具有我方背
   書的第二張滙票才予付
   款。

3.滙票背書 Endorsement

　　滙票的背書（endorsement）就是在滙票背面簽名，將所有權轉讓給他人的意思。其中有 1.只需要背書人（endorser）簽名，而不需寫上被背書人（endorsee）姓名者—— 即**空白背書**（blank endorsement）。 2.寫下被背書人姓名並經持票人簽名者—— 即**完全背書**（full endorsement）。 3.指定被背書人（to order of ～）並由背書人簽名— 即**指定背書**（endorsement to order），稱爲指定滙票（order bill），在任何場合都具有流通性（negotiability）。背書時，2.的完全背書需在滙票背面寫上 **Please pay the sum due on the bill**〔滙票金額〕**to x**，並由背書人簽名。3.的指定滙票也一樣要寫上 **Please pay the sum due on the bill to order of** x，再由背書人簽名。1.則只需背書人簽名即可。

滙 票 背 書 必 備 例 句

A. 完全背書（Full Endorsement）

1. You will find an enclosed draft for $500 on the First National Bank, New York, *endorsed in your favor*.

　　茲附寄以貴方爲受款人，紐約的第一國民銀行，五百元的背書滙票，請查收。

2. Enclosed is a draft for $500 on the First National Bank, New York, *endorsed in your favor*.

　　茲隨函奉寄以貴方爲背書，開給紐約的第一國民銀行，五百元的滙票一張。

B. 指定背書（To Order of Endorsee）

1. We enclose First of Exchange Demand Draft on London, No. 30 for £2,000, *endorsed to your order*.

   茲附上指定讓渡給貴方的背書滙票，編號30二千英鎊的倫敦第一張即期滙票。

2. Today we sent you an enclosed draft on the New York Bank for $2,000, *endorsed to your order*, which you will please find in order.

   今天本公司附寄一張指定讓渡給貴方的背書滙票開給紐約銀行面額二千元，敬請查收。

C. 空白背書（Blank Endorsement）

1. We are pleased to send you an enclosed draft on Bank of Taiwan, New York, for $2,000, *endorsed in blank*.

   茲隨函奉寄空白背書，開給紐約的台灣銀行，面額二千元的滙票。

2. We return you the draft on account of *omitted endorsement*, and feel obliged if you will send back the same, *endorsed in blank*.

   茲寄還貴方的滙票，因爲背書被刪除，若蒙寄回空白背書的同樣滙票，則不勝感激。

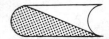 滙 票 須 知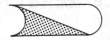

1. 開票用句 draw **upon** you, value **on** you 的 on、upon 表付款，
後面接付款人或付款地。

  paper on Taipei 台北付款的滙票（ paper ＝滙票、證券）

2. **surrender the documents**「交付裝運文件」，documents 指
的是 shipping documents.

3. 發信用句，**in favor of** 之後接押滙銀行,因其已代進口商墊付。
in favor of ～意思爲「以～爲抬頭或受款人」。

4. 議付滙票的銀行即押滙銀行，亦即接受滙票金額的人。

  We draw on you **through** the A Bank.

  由A銀行開出滙票給您。

介系詞不用 at，應採「經由，受理」之意的 through。就如「由
A銀行開立L/C」的 We opened an L/C **with** the A Bank.
其介系詞不用 at 而用 with一樣，要特別注意。

5. **an acceptance** 已承兌滙票

6. enclosed **with** the letter 或 enclosed **in** the letter 或 advised
in the letter 或 advised **by** the letter 之用法如下：

(a) A cheque is enclosed ***with*** the letter.

(b) A cheque is enclosed ***in the*** letter.

  (a)是正確的，但若考慮到是包括信文的 letter，也可以用(b)，
  總之，兩者都對。

(c) as per advice ***in*** your letter.

(d) as per advised ***by*** your letter.

(c)表在「信文中」 (d)表「藉由信件」之意，兩者皆可。

7. **for account of** 「以(某人)的帳戶(支付)」，通常其後接進口商之名，即付款人為進口商。

8. **take up the bill** 承兌、支付滙票

9. **protect, honor** 支付、承兌滙票

10. **the bill was dishonored** 這張滙票遭退票

11. 見票即付 D/P 滙票 sight D/P, D/P draft at sight
    見票後六十日付款 D/P 滙票 60 d/s D/P, D/P draft at 60 d/s
    見票後六十日付款 D/A 滙票 60 d/s D/A, D/A draft at 60 d/s

12. **due〔on〕August** 30 應於 8 月 30 日付款 (到期)
    payable〔on〕August 30 同上
    (due = payable 應支付，到期的)
    due date, date of maturity 到期日
    The draft matures on August 30.
    滙票於 8 月 30 日到期。
    the amount due at maturity 到期日應支付金額

13. **Please find the acceptance in order.**「請查收已承兌滙票。」
    find ～ in order 是由「確定其完全無誤」之意引申而為中文的「請查收，請查驗」之意。

14. to **endorse** the draft **in one's favor,** the draft **endorsed in one's favor** 「以～為受款人在滙票上背書」

15. the draft **endorsed to one's order**「指定讓渡給某人的背書滙票」

16. **demand draft** 即期滙票 (= sight draft)

17. the funds we hold at your disposal
按照您的指示我方可以處理的現款

18. the sum **due** on the bill（draft） 匯票面額

19. 美元＝US＄ USD（電傳）
英鎊＝stg£ STGL（電傳）
五十美元 US＄50 五十英鎊 stg£50

20. 以貴方名義付款的匯票 a bill payable in your name

21. **payee**「受款人，被支付人」
the payee of a draft「匯票的受款人」

22. an accountee 帳戶受款人

【說明】 名詞的字尾 ee 表「接受某行為的人」，例如
examin**ee**, employ**ee**, inquir**ee**, appoint**ee**, nomin**ee**,
etc.

滙 票 模 範 書 信

A. 開出滙票（Drawing of Draft）

1

Today we have ***drawn on*** you, ***for account of***
Messrs. Edmond Hamilton & Co., New York, N.Y., ***in***
favor of the First Commercial Bank, Taipei, by 30
d/s for invoice amount of ＄10,000 covering your order No. 150 for 100 bales of cotton products. The
draft was drawn under the irrevocable letter of

credit No. 1500 issued by the National Bank of New York, N.Y. ***Kindly protect the draft upon presentation***.

今天我方以紐約艾德蒙・漢米爾頓公司為付款人，以台北的第一商業銀行為抬頭，開給貴方發票總額一萬元，見票三十天支付的滙票，以抵償貴方第 150 號，一百綑綿製品的訂單。本滙票是以紐約的國民銀行發行的第 1500 號不可撤銷信用狀為本所開的。請在提出時加以承兌。

2

Today we have drawn on you by 30d/s, ***as agreed***, for ***invoice value*** of $5,000, under irrevocable letter of credit No. 2,300 issued by the Bank of America, New York City, New York, and ***negotiated*** the draft ***through*** the Taipei Branch of the same Bank, which you will please note.

今天本公司以紐約市美國銀行發行的第 2300 號不可撤銷信用狀為本，依貴方所同意的，開出發票面額五千元，見票三十天支付的滙票，敬請注意，本滙票是經由同一家銀行台北分行押滙的。

B. 支付、承兌、拒絕滙票（Payment, Acceptance & Refusal of Draft）

1

We are pleased to advise you that your draft for £2,000 *in favor of* Mr. P. Melford has been duly *presented* and *honored* to the debit of your account.

您以梅爾弗德先生爲抬頭，面額二千英鎊的滙票，已經即時提示，並已兌現爲貴方借項，特此奉告。

2

We are pleased to inform you that we have *accepted* your draft for $1,000 *in favor of* John Smith & Co., to which reference was made in your letter of June 15.

敬告貴方，本公司已經承兌您以約翰·史密斯公司爲抬頭，面額一千元的滙票，請查詢貴方 7 月 15 日來函。

3

It is with deep regret that we find ourselves unable to meet *in full* our acceptance No. 3310 which *falls due* on December 20, and we trust you will appreciate our difficulty. We should be very grateful if you would take Stg £1,000 *in cash* and a further three months' bill for the *balance*, together with interest thereon at 7.5 percent.

發現本公司第3310號，12月20日到期的承兌滙票無法全數支付，深以爲憾，相信貴方會體諒本公司的困難。如果貴方願收現金一千英鎊，餘額以三個月的支票，及百分之七點五的利息付款，則不勝感激。

4

Your refusal to honor your acceptance for £2,000 *in our favor* has greatly surprised us and your action is all the more reprehensible in the absence of any *intimation* that dishonor was likely. And now, we have no alternative but to insist on a cash payment within three days, *in default of which* legal proceedings will be unavoidable.

　　貴方拒絕如期支付本公司受款，面額二千英鎊的承兌滙票，使本公司大爲驚訝，貴方未予通告，因之可能遭退票的行爲更應該受責備。現在，本公司別無選擇，只能堅持三天之內以現金付款，若不履行債務，採取法律訴訟是不可避免的。

➡ reprehensible〔ˌrɛprɪˈhɛnsəbl̩〕*adj.* 應受責備的

➡ intimation〔ˌɪntəˈmeʃən〕*n.* 通告

➡ default〔dɪˈfɔlt〕*n.*〔法律〕不履行債務

5

Very much to our surprise, Messrs. Mansfield & Co. refuse to ***honor*** their acceptance for £2,000 ***due on*** March 23, explaining that they had been advised that the bill had been stolen from Messrs. Peel, of Winchester. As the bill appeared to be quite ***in order*** when you endorsed it to us, we must ask you to see that our interests are in no way ***prejudiced***.

　　曼斯菲爾公司拒付面額二千英鎊，3月23日到期的承兌滙票，使我方大爲驚訝，他們的解釋是曾經被通知該票在文契斯特皮爾公司被竊。因爲當貴方背書給本公司時，該票顯然完全無誤，敬請貴方了解我方的利益絕不容受損害。

➡ prejudice〔ˈprɛdʒədɪs〕*v.* 損害（利益、權利等）

第9章
訂貨之付款及催收
Payment for Order & Dunning

　　在貿易上貨款的支付，有每次交易每次付清的情況，但大部分都是按月或定期（例如每季）執行。在船貨上一定要附 Invoice ，到預定的總計時期，出口商會將**結算清單**（ **statement of account** ——也可單用 **statement** ）寄來。其中，包括買賣當事人之間的收支結算（ balance ）進口商便依此 statement 付款。若到期還未支付，就必須發出催款單（ reminder ），第一封催款單可以平和的口吻，詢問對方是否失察（ oversight ），若仍不付款時，就要漸漸加重口氣，最後則需威脅（ threat ）訴諸法律途徑（ legal step ）的意圖。Statement of Account 的信件及型式如下：

〔例〕

Dear Sirs,

We are sending the enclosed Statement of Account for your orders of last month, and please examine it. If you find it in order, kindly make remittance at your early convenience.

Yours sincerely,

〔樣本〕 **STATEMANT OF ACCOUNT**的範例

STATEMENT

5 Hsin Yang Street,

Taipei, May 31st, 1986

Messrs. James Atkinson & Co.

New York

$ 468,000

Date	Particulars	Unit Price	Amount
Apr. 5	3 Olympia Typewriters	$80,000	$240,000
Apr. 15	2 doz. Typewriter Ribbon	$ 200	$ 48,000
Apr. 30	2 Olivetti Typewriters	$90,000	$180,000
		Total	$468,000

E. & O. E.

Taiwan International Stationery Co.

(signed)

Manager

【說明】 1. 一般都將索帳者的地址寫於日期之前。

2. *E.&O.E.* 是 *Errors and Omissions Excepted* 之略，意爲「有錯當查；錯誤遺漏不在此限」，是爲了保留日後修改的權利，也常用於 Invoice 。

付 款 及 催 收 必 備 例 句

A. 付款通知（ Advice of Payment ）

1. Today, we *paid* $~ for our orders *into your account* at ~ Bank.

   今天本公司將訂單金額～元付淸，記入貴方在～銀行的帳戶。

2. Today we are sending a draft enclosed for US$~ on the X Bank, *endorsed in your favor.*

   玆寄上以貴方爲受款人，X 銀行美金～元背書滙票一張。

3. We take pleasure in sending you a cheque of US$~ *in full* (*part*) *settlement of your account.*

   很樂意奉寄美金～元的支票，全數（部分）支付貴方的帳款。

4. Enclosed is a cheque for US$~ *in full* (*part*) *settlement of your account.*

   玆附上美金～元支票一張，以全數（部分）支付貴方的帳款。

5. We have today instructed our bankers...to remit the *amount due* by cable.

   今天本公司已發電報指示…銀行滙寄到期的金額。

   ➡ remit〔rɪˈmɪt〕 *n.* 滙寄

6. We have arranged payment of your
   invoice No. 500 for the goods
   received. Kindly acknowledge receipt on *entering the money to
   your credit*.

   已經收到貴方貨品，並
   已安排支付貴方第 500
   號發票之事宜。錢一進
   帳敬請來函告知。

   ➡ acknowledge〔ək'nɑlɪdʒ〕v. 致函或宣布收到

7. Please receive the sum *on account*.

   請收下本金額做爲部分
   付款。

   ➡ *on account* 做爲部分（分期）付款

8. We are pleased to enclose our
   cheque for £2,000 in settlement
   of your statement of account
   dated May 30, covering our *orders for April*.

   很樂於奉寄二千英鎊的
   支票，以支付貴方 5 月
   30 日對本公司 4 月訂
   單提出的結算清單。

9. In the circumstances, we trust
   you will accept our cheque for
   £1,000 *on account, subject to
   payment of the balance* next
   month.

   於此情況下，相信以下
   個月付清餘額爲條件，
   貴方會接受本公司一千
   英鎊的支票，做爲部分
   付款。

B. 請求付款（Request for Payment）

1. May we ask you to *remit* us US
   $500 covering your order of May
   3rd?

   敬請滙款美金五百元給
   本公司，以支付貴方 5
   月 3 日的訂單。

2. *May we draw your attention to* our statement dated May 3rd for the total amount of Stg£2,500 covering your orders for April?

敬請注意本公司5月3日對貴方4月的訂單所提出的，總額二千五百英鎊的結算清單。

3. May we ask you for *prompt clearance* of all *invoiced accounts*?

敬請儘速付清所有的發票帳款。

4. Enclosed is a statement of your *account for the goods* ordered.

茲奉寄貴方所訂貨物的結算清單。

5. We must draw your attention to your *outstanding money* (account).

敬請注意未付的錢（帳款）。

　➡ outstanding〔aut'stændɪŋ〕*adj.* 未付的

6. *May we remind you of* your *long-overdue account on our books*?

提請貴方注意我方帳簿上，您過期很久的帳款。

7. *May we remind you that the amount due*, as per last statement *rendered*, has not yet been paid?

提請貴方，照上次提出的結算清單，金額已到期，但尚未付款。

8. We *regret the necessity of reminding you of* your unpaid bill of £2,000 now *three months overdue*.

抱歉必須提醒貴方，未付的二千英鎊支票，現已過期三個月了。

　➡ *remind one of* ～ 提醒（某人）～

9. We regret that your *account of* £1,000 has been so long outstanding.

貴方一千英鎊的帳款日久未付，深以為憾。

10. We deeply regret that you have not shown us *the courtesy of replying* to our two previous requests for payment of your *accounts with us* now three months overdue.

貴方對於本公司前兩次要求付清，現已過期三個月的欠款，未惠予答覆，使我方深以為憾。

11. We must insist on payment within seven days, *failing which* we shall be obliged to *proceed against you*.

本公司必須堅持貴方在七日內付款，否則將不得不控訴貴方。

➡ proceed〔prə'sid〕*v*.〔法律〕控訴

12. We enclose the statement of account up to April 30 showing a *balance* in our favor of $1,000 and hope to receive a cheque in settlement *in due course*.

茲奉寄到4月30日為止的結算清單，可以看出我方應得一千元的差額，希望不久能收到付款的支票。

➡ *in due course* 不久終將

13. We thank you for your letter enclosing a cheque in part-payment of your account, but would point out that *the sum still outstanding is considerable*.

感謝貴方來函中附寄一張支票以部分付清帳款，但是我方要指出，未付的數目仍然相當龐大。

14. We are ***working on a small-profit basis***, so the ***long-drawn payment of your account with us*** would be fatal to us minor traders.

我方本著小額利潤經營，所以貴方將欠款開得這麼久，對我方這樣的小貿易商乃致命傷。

15. You may have ***overlooked*** our statement of April 30, otherwise the account must have been paid by now.

貴方可能忽略了本公司 4 月 30 日的清單，否則現在帳款應已付清才對。

16. We are surprised that you have taken no notice of our two previous ***applications*** for a settlement of our ***account of*** $2,000, which is now much overdue, our terms being 30 days from the date of invoice.

貴方對於本公司前兩次申請付清二千元帳款，未予注意，使我方大為驚訝。以從發票日起三十天付款的條件，該筆款項現已過期良久。

請求付款的結尾語

1. We shall appreciate your giving this your immediate ***attention.***

若蒙立刻處理此事，不勝感激。

2. We look forward to your prompt ***remittance.***

期待貴方即時滙款。

3. Looking forward to your prompt reply and trusting to ***be favored with*** your early ***remittance***,

期待貴方即時答覆，相信有幸早日收到滙款。

4. We regret that your failure to settle your account by July 3rd has left us with no alternative but to demand payment by return of post, or *institute legal proceedings in the event of default*.

很遺憾貴方未能在7月3日前付清帳款，使我方沒有選擇餘地，只能要求以回郵付款，萬一不履行則提出法律訴訟。

➡ by return of post 以回郵

➡ institute 〔'ɪnstə,tjut 〕 *v*. 提出 (訴訟)

5. *Your usual early settlement will be appreciated.*

如依往常儘早付款，不勝感激。

C. 延期付款〔 Grace (Extension) of Payment 〕

1. If you will grant us *a few days' grace (extension)*, we promise to pay in full our account with you.

若蒙貴方寬容幾天，本公司答應付清全額帳款。

2. We shall be glad if you will kindly allow your account to *stand over* till April 20.

若蒙貴方允許延至4月20日付款，則不勝感激。

➡ *stand over* 延長：延期

3. We suppose that your draft on Messrs. Henderson & Co., if attended with *sixty days' grace*, may be complied with to the full.

本公司認為貴方開給韓德森公司的滙票，若能惠予延長六十天，可以被應允付清全額。

4. Fortunately, we had the allowance of 10 *days' grace* for payment.

很幸運地，本公司被應允延後十天付款。

5. As we are unable to meet your draft for $1,000 due at the end of this month, we are *under the necessity of* requesting you to *renew the same* for three months.

因爲本公司無法支付貴方這個月底到期，面額一千元的滙票，因此必須要求將該票據延後三個月。

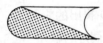 付 款 及 催 收 須 知

1. **overdue** 〔'ovə'dju〕 *adj.* 過期的
   overdue bill 過期的滙票

2. **outstanding** 〔aut'stændɪŋ〕 *adj.* 未付的

3. **on account** 做爲部分付款；做爲分期付款

4. **amount due(payable)** 應支付的金額

5. **ACCOUNT & BALANCE** （借貸關係）的用法
   your account *with* us ⟶ the account you owe us
     貴方的債務
   your account *against* us ⟶ the account we owe you
     貴方的債權
   our account *with* you ⟶ the account we owe you
     我方的債務
   our account *against* you ⟶ the account you owe us
     我方的債權

with = advantageous to ∼

against = disadvantageous to ∼

our account *with* the bank ──→ our deposit *in the hands of* the bank 我方在銀行的存款

the balance due 應付的餘額 → 不足額

the balance *due(to) us* is ＄50 應付給我方五十元的餘額

a balance *in our favor* of ＄50 同上

your cheque *to balance* your account with us

清償貴方債務的貴方發行支票

the account *rendered* up to (date) 到（日期）提出的帳單

the account *for* the past two months 過去兩個月的帳單

our account *of* ＄1,000 我方一千元的帳單

the account *on* the cotton products of our order

我方棉製品訂單的帳單

6. *value* of orders 訂購貨物的總值

   in replacement *of* ∼ 以代替∼

   replacements *of* ∼ ∼的代替品

7. Surrender 和 Realize 的意義

   Shipping documents were *surrendered* to the consignee.
   裝運文件交付給收件人。

   The business was just *realized*. 商談剛剛達成。

   His assets were *realized*. 他的資產變賣成現金。

8. 延期的種種說法

   grace (extension) of payment 延期付款

   grace means a delay allowed as a favor, as for *payment*, *work*, *etc*.

1) There are three days of *grace* allowed for payment.

　　容許延緩三天付款。

2) I'll give you a week's *grace*, but if the work is not finished then, you'll be punished. 我將給你一週的寬限，

　　但是如果到那時工作尚未完成，你會受罰。

renew the draft 更新滙票期限；延長滙票期限

stand over 延長；延期

1) We have decided to stand over his payment for a week.

　　我方已決定讓他的付款延長一星期。

2) The meeting stood over to another date.

　　會議延期到另一天。

days of grace 延遲付款的期間

　　** 交貨期限延長 extension (grace) of delivery

9. **in due course** ⟶ without too much delay

　　不久終將；到適當的時候

10. **an application, a reminder** 申請書，催討書。催討書也可以說

　　成 dunning letter 或 demand letter。

訂　貨　之　付　款　及　催　收　模　範　書　信

A. 支付訂貨 (Payment for Order)

1

The goods *invoiced* by you on April 15 have now

safely arrived and are satisfactory. In settlement of

the amount of your invoice, *less* 5 percent discount, we enclose a sight draft, value \$1,000, which you will please *find correct*.

貴方 4月15日開發票的貨物現在已安全抵達，而且很令人滿意。茲附上見票即付的滙票，面額一千元，以支付貴方發票的金額，減去百分之五的折扣，盼查核無誤。

【說明】 invoice 作動詞是由「寄送發票，結帳」引申為「連帶寄送發票」之意。

2

We enclose a cheque, value \$1,500, which with 2 per-cent reduction, *balances your account* up to and in-cluding April 20. As the other *items on your state-ment* are after this date, they *fall due* only on June 1, according to usual terms. Please, therefore, bring them forward to the next account. We hope the cheque will be found in order. (*or*, An acknowledge-ment of the cheque will be appreciated.)

茲附上支票一張，扣除百分之二後，總值一千五百元，以結算到 4月20日（當天包括在內）的帳單。因為貴方結算清單的其他項目，在此日期之後，依照一般條款，於 6月1日才到期。因此，請將它們列入下期的帳單。盼支票查收無誤。（ 或，若來函告知收到支票，則不勝感激。）

B. 請求付款（Request for Payment）

1

May we respectfully call your attention to the enclosed *statement*? As we have some very *heavy payments to meet* this month, we should be greatly obliged if you would let us have a cheque.

敬請注意附寄的結算清單。因爲本公司這個月須支付一些非常重要的款項，若蒙貴方惠予支票，則不勝感激。

2

We should like to remind you that *the amount due,* as in our statement *rendered*, has not yet been paid, and we shall be grateful by your remitting this at your earliest convenience.

提醒貴方本公司提出的結算清單上，到期的金額尚未支付，若蒙貴方儘早滙款，則不勝感激。

3

We wish to call your attention to *our account of* \$1,000, which has *evidently escaped your notice*. We

shall be glad if you will let us have by return your
cheque *to balance this*.

望貴方注意本公司一千元的帳單，貴方顯然忽略了。若貴方接到信
立刻給本公司支票，以結算這筆帳款，則深感幸甚。

➡ by return 立刻；接到信之後

4

We have already written twice to remind you of your
delinquent account with us, but are still willing to assume that your case may be *one of overlooking, rather
than of disregarding*, our requests. You can easily
prove our assumption correct by sending us at once,
·in the enclosed return envelope, your cheque for the
amount in full that you owe. Won't you act now?

本公司已經寫兩封信提醒貴方拖欠我方的帳款，但仍然願意假定可
能是貴方疏忽了，而不是不理睬本公司的要求。貴方可以立刻將欠本公
司的全額支票，裝入附寄的回郵信封寄回，以證明我方的假定是正確的。
請現在採取行動。

➡ delinquent〔dɪ'lɪŋkwənt〕*adj.* 拖欠的；違法的

第10章
代理實務・委託銷售
Agency; Consignment

A. 代理店實務（Agency）

代理店（Agency）的實務是行代理行為及代理權。依據國外本店（principal）的意思，代行銷售行為，從中取得一定的佣金，這就是所謂的**代理商**（agent），實為買賣的中間商。代理銷售者是 selling agent，代理購買者是 buying agent。依本店請託在國外購買稱為 Indent（受託購買者），在第二章「出價」和第四章「訂購關係」中都已提過，不再贅敘。

selling agent 可分為 **sole（exclusive）selling agent（獨家銷售代理商或總代理商）**及 **non-exclusive selling agent（非獨占性銷售代理商）**兩種。前者屬於在一國或廣大區域內擁有獨家銷售權或獨占銷售權者，後者則是在同一地區有數家代理店，以限制獨占權。這些代理商都獨占或非獨占性地代行本店的銷售行為，和本店有極端密切的關係，必須與本店締結代理合同（Agency Agreement）。代理合同內容包括

代理權限、銷售地區、經銷商品、價格標準、抽成率、滙款方式及合同之有效期限等等。買賣契約是由本店與當地顧客直接締結的，信用狀也以此原則開發給顧客，貨品由本店直接送達顧客處，當然滙票也是由本店向顧客提出。

代理商原則上是透過目錄、樣本等，搜集當地的訂單及銷售預約。出口時的價格都採 CIF & C ， FOB & C ，即包括 commission（佣金）的價格，然後，本店再定期整理 commission，以「回佣（ return commission ）」方式匯款給代理商。另一種方式如同模範書信開頭的例句一樣，直接收取物品銷售，然後再將寄銷清單（ Account Sales — 後述 ）寄送本人；也就是併用了委託銷售的方式。但，從嚴格的觀點來看，代理實務還是如前所述的，代理人主要從事搜集訂單，辦理銷售預約的工作，佣金以「回佣」方式取得為原則。

世界貿易中大部分都以 Agency Agreement 進行。在陌生的地域尋求銷路時，任命精通當地情況的代理店，開拓、擴大銷路，以提高出口實績，是相當聰明的作法。在此必須注意，為了進口商而設的進口中間商（非代理），和本店之間關係淡薄，不是在當地為本店而活動的，所以不能稱之為代理店。代理店必須以本店身份代行本店的利益。此外，也別將**銷售代理商**（ selling agent ）和**銷售商**（ distributor ）混淆。銷售商是將本店送達的貨品，以自己的帳戶和姓名購入銷售，所以對本店來說是站在 principal to principal（本店對本店）的地位。此外，本店和銷售商訂的契約是 Distributorship Agreement ，這和本店與銷售代理店訂的 Agency Agreement 是不同的。

B. 委託銷售（ Consignment Sales ）

這兒所談的**委託銷售**（ sales on commission ; consignment sales ）是指國外貿易中的委託形態一項。由於情況特殊，所以必須得

到經濟部的許可。身爲委託者(consignor)的出口商不和受託者(consignee)訂立買賣契約，只訂託售合同(Consignment Agreement)，商品直接發往國外的批發商(Commission House)或國外貿易公司，請求他們銷售。在貨物裝船之後，立刻將寄售發票(consignment invoice)寄給受託者。收到貨品的受託者就與當地顧客訂立買賣契約，委託貨品售完之後，按照託售合同的規定，將售款扣掉手續費、墊款及各種費用之後的寄銷清單(Account Sales — A/S)寄給委託者，這種方式經常用於**開拓新市場**或**推銷新產品**的時候。託售貿易是委託國外的第三者銷售，風險較大，所以如前所述的，必須得到政府許可。以下將代理店貿易、託售貿易及銷售店的商務以圖表示之。

1. 代理店貿易

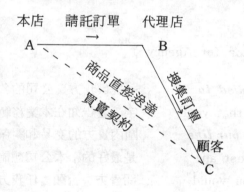

ＡＢ可視爲一體，Ａ與Ｃ直接訂立買賣契約。

2. 委託銷售貿易

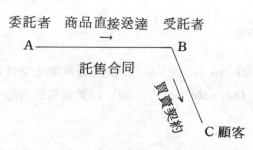

ＡＢ訂立託售合同，但不訂立買賣契約。ＢＣ則訂立買賣契約。Ａ與Ｃ無直接關係。

3. 銷售店的商務

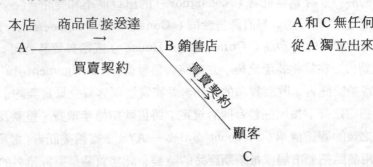

本店　商品直接送達
→
A ——————— B 銷售店
買賣契約
買賣契約

A和C無任何關係。B
從A獨立出來。

顧客
C

代 理 · 委 託 必 備 例 句

A. 代理店實務（ Agency ）

a) 代理權之申請（ Application for Agency ）

1. Your name has been ***supplied to*** us by...who informs us that your trade and connections in ***our line of business*** are of the best and we wish to inquire if you would ***be disposed to*** appoint us as your agent.

　➡ ***be disposed to*** 想要；有意

…提供我方貴公司的名字，並告知在本業務範圍內貴方的交易和關係是最好的，本公司想詢問貴方是否願委任我方為代理商。

2. We hear that you require an a-gent in this town ***for the sale of*** your goods.

聽說貴方徵求本地代理商，以銷售您的貨品。

3. As our *influence* here would undoubtedly be greater than in any other place, we hope that you can *appoint* us as your agent.

因爲本公司在此地的影響力，無疑地比在任何地方大，因此希望貴方能委任本公司做代理商。

4. Should you be inclined to *entertain* our offer, kindly write us conditions upon which you would appoint us your agent.

若您有意考慮本公司的提議，請寫信告知您願委任我方爲代理商的條件。

➡ entertain〔,ɛntə'ten〕*v.* 考慮；心存

5. Hearing from a friend that you are in want of an agent in Taiwan for the sale of *your style of goods*, we wish to *offer our services*.

從朋友處聽說貴方需要一家在台代理商，以銷售貴方款式的貨物，本公司願意效勞。

➡ *be in want of* 需要

6. In view of the *wide connections* which we are fortunate enough to possess, we think you will agree that a 5 percent *commission on* net sales is quite reasonable. Also we are prepared to guarantee the payment of all accounts.

鑑於本公司有幸擁有廣濶的關係，相信貴方會同意淨銷售額百分之五的傭金是相當合理的。本公司也準備保證一切賒欠的支付。

7. The excellent reputation which *your house* enjoys here *renders us* extremely *desirous of entering*, if possible, *into business relations with you.*

　　➡ *enter into* 締結（關係、協約等）

貴行在此地享有的盛名，使本公司亟欲和貴行締結交易關係，如果可能的話。

8. If you are not yet *represented* in this region, we would inquire whether you would be pleased to accept us as your *agent for this territory.*

　　➡ territory〔'tɛrə,torɪ〕*n.* 地方；領域

若貴方在本區尚無代理店，請問是否樂意接受我方爲本地代理店。

9. If you are desirous of extending your business relations in this country, we should be pleased to *enter into an agreement with you* to act as *your representatives* here.

若貴方有意在本國擴展交易關係，本公司很樂意和貴方締結合同，充當您此地的代理店。

10. We wish to offer you our services for any purchases *you may have to make* in this market.

對於貴方在本地市場可能必須做的採購，本公司希望能爲您效勞。

11. This region offers a splendid *field* for the disposal of your goods.

本地對貴方貨品的銷售提供絕佳的市場。

12. It seems to us that there is a *fair opening* in this country for the sale of your new products and we should be happy to act as your agent in this matter, should you be *disposed to entertain the idea*.

我方認爲貴公司新產品的銷售在本國有相當好的機會。如果貴方顧意考慮這個想法，本公司樂意充當您的代理商。

13. Apparently you are not repre-sented here, and *it occurs to us* that if you had a regular agent, your business would be consider-ably increased.

顯然貴方在此地尙無代理商，本公司想到，若您有固定代理商，生意必定大增。

14. We wish to advise you that *ours is a house* with many years' busi-ness background in this place and has not only a thorough knowledge of *the class of goods in which you deal*, but also is well ac-quainted with a large number of *prospective buyers* in this local-ity.

希望告知貴方，本行在此地有多年的商務經歷，不僅對貴方經營的貨品類別有深入的知識，而且熟識本地許多可能的買主。

➡ prospective〔prə'spɛktɪv〕*adj.* 可能的；有望的

15. Having been established many years, we have good connections *throughout the trade*.

本公司成立多年，在整個貿易界有很好的關係。

16. Our *experience* and *local knowledge* will enable us to give you entire satisfaction whenever you may require our services.

以本公司的經驗和對本地市場的了解，無論何時貴方需要我方效勞，都會使您完全滿意。

17. As our *connections throughout the whole of the Taiwan market* are numerous, a large annual *turnover* would *result*, should you *see your way to* appointing us as your agent here.

因爲本公司在整個台灣市場上，有無數關係，如果貴方能委任本公司爲此地代理商，每年必會達到大量營業額。

➡ turnover〔'tɜn,ovə〕 *n.* 營業額

18. If you *entrust us with* the responsibility for your agency, *you may rest assured that* we should make every endeavor to further your interests, to our mutual profit and satisfaction.

若蒙您將代理的責任委託給本公司，您可以確信，爲了雙方的利潤和均感滿意，我方將盡全力增進貴方的利益。

➡ entrust〔ɪn'trʌst〕 *v.* 委託

19. There is a lively demand for the smaller type of electric household appliances in our town and we are keen to assist you to *get your productions known here.*

本地對小型家電製品需求頗大，我方熱切協助貴方，使您的產品打開這裡的知名度。

➡ appliance〔ə'plaɪəns〕 *n.* 用具

20. We hear that you have not yet been represented in our country. May we *venture to announce ourselves as a candidate* for a *sole agency* for your lines in which we are deeply interested. Ours is an export and import house dealing mainly in machinery and electric parts and having a business background of 30 years.

  聽說貴方在本國尚無代理店。本行想冒昧自薦，爲貴方產品的獨家代理店的候選人。我方對該產品深感興趣。本行主要經營機械和電氣零件的進出口，商務經歷達三十年。

 ➡ sole agency 獨家代理權

21. Should you decide to *entrust* the representation of your firm *to* us, we would make it our business to *guard your interests* to the best of our ability.

  貴方若決定委託我方爲代理店，本公司會竭盡所能，以保護貴方的利益爲職責所在。

22. We feel certain that we should be able to give you satisfaction, *attending to* your interests in such a manner as to give you no cause to regret having put them into our hands.

  本公司抱持不使貴方後悔委託我方的態度，來爲貴方的利益服務，一定能令您感到滿意。

23. You can be sure that any orders you may send us will be executed at the most *favorable market prices*.

  貴方可以確信，本公司會以最有利的市場價格，履行您寄來的任何訂單。

b) 提供代理權；對申請代理店的答覆
(Offer of Agency; Reply to Agency Applicant)

1. We are pleased to state that we are prepared to appoint you our agent for Norfolk and Suffolk *on a commission basis of* 5 percent with hotel, traveling and *miscellaneous* expenses.

很高興通知貴方，本公司準備委派貴方，爲諾福克郡和沙福克郡的代理商，包括旅館、旅遊和其他雜費在內，傭金百分之五。

➡ miscellaneous〔 ˌmɪslˈenɪəs 〕*adj.* 繁雜的；各種的

2. We realize also that the special features of your territory demand that we should *leave* a great deal *to your discretion* in such matters as discounts and terms of credit *to be allowed*. Provided therefore that your arrangements do not seriously *prejudice our interests*, we propose to *give you a free hand*.

本公司也了解貴地需求的特色，故很多事情將由貴方自行處理，像答應折扣和信用狀條件之類。因此倘若貴方的安排不致嚴重損及我方的利益，本公司打算授予您處理上之完全自由。

➡ *free hand* 處理上之完全自由

3. You will realize that we are placing a great deal of confidence in you and we trust that your weekly *returns* will justify our estimate of your ability.

貴方應了解本公司對您非常信任，相信貴方每週的收益，將會證明我方對您能力的估量是正確的。

4. We should like to appoint you our sole New York agent *for a period of twelve months from date*, and agree to pay you a commission of 2 percent on all orders received direct or indirect from New York buyers.

本公司想指派貴方爲紐約獨家代理商，從卽日起爲期十二個月，並同意付所有從紐約買主直接、或間接收到的訂單之百分之二做傭金。

5. Our products are so popular in any market that you will soon be able to do business big enough to let us consider giving you easier terms and *granting* you the *sole agency* in your country.

本公司產品在任何市場皆受歡迎，因此貴方很快卽能達成大筆交易。屆時我方會考慮給貴方更便利的條件，並應允您在貴國的獨家代理權。

  ➡ sole agency 獨家代理權

6. We have received your letter of June 5 and have taken your offer to act as our agent, *with exclusive rights for* India, into serious consideration.

6月5日來函敬悉，並已愼重考慮貴方擔任本公司在印度獨家代理商的提議。

  ➡ exclusive〔ɪkˈsklusɪv〕*adj.* 獨佔的

7. We are very much interested to receive your kind offer to represent us at Bombay *on a commission basis*.

本公司接到您好意提議，以傭金制度，做我方孟買代理商，深感興趣。

  ➡ *on a commission basis* 基於傭金制度

8. After thorough consideration of your proposal, we have decided to appoint you our *sole Bombay agent*.

詳細考慮此提案後，本公司決定指派貴方，為孟買獨家代理商。

9. We wish to notify you that after *due consideration* of the proposal contained in your last letter, we are prepared to offer you our agency *upon the following terms*.

在慎重考慮貴方前封信的提議後，本公司準備基於下列條件，提供我方的代理權，特此奉告。

10. Please let us know what commission you are prepared to accept.

請通知本公司貴方準備接受多少傭金。

11. The whole matter *hinges upon* the question of the amount of commission you would require on *orders obtained and executed*.

整件事視貴方在獲得和履行訂單上，對傭金數額要求的問題而定。

➡ hinge〔hɪndʒ〕*v.* 依…而定

12. We are afraid we cannot appoint an agent in your city as the returns would not be sufficient to *repay us for the expense involved*.

本公司恐怕不能在貴城指派代理商，因為收益不夠不足以抵付有關的費用。

13. Please *let us know* at once if this meets with your approval.

若本案獲貴方同意，請立刻告知。

14. We have the pleasure of stating below our business terms and, if you find them acceptable, please have kindness to confirm *by return mail*.

很高興載明雙方交易條件如下，如果貴方認爲可以接受，接到信後請立刻確認。

15. We trust you will *fall in with* the above general conditions and shall be glad to hear your views.

相信貴方會同意上述的一般條件，期待接到回音。

   ➡ *fall in with* 同意

16. We have had many offers, but there always seemed to be too great a *risk* involved, since we could not be assured that the *consignments* we might send would find a market, and there appeared every probability that our goods would either be *sold off* at a considerable loss or returned *as unsalable*.

本公司曾接到多份提案，但是既然不能確保我方託售的物品，找得到市場，而且我方貨品，很可能不是以相當大的虧損廉價出售，就是賣不出去被退還，似乎總是牽涉到很大的風險。

   ➡ *sell off* 廉價出售

17. A *del credere commission* of 2.5 percent would also be allowed if you would be prepared to accept it.

若貴方準備接受，本公司可以同意百分之二點五的保證收取貨款傭金。

   ➡ *del credere commission* 保證收取貨款傭金

18. We are willing to allow you an extra commission of 2.5 percent for *del credere*, as we could not *risk any losses through bad debts*.

    ➡ bad debt 呆帳

本公司不能因爲呆帳而冒任何虧損的危險，故意給貴方保證收取貨款百分之二點五的額外傭金。

19. Our allowance towards your office expenses shall be $5,000 per annum *payable quarterly* with your commission.

    ➡ per annum 每年
    ➡ quarterly〔'kwɔrtəlɪ〕*adv*. 一年四次地；每季地

本公司給貴方業務經費津貼每年五千元，與貴方的傭金一併一年分四次付款。

提供代理權，對申請代理店的答覆結尾語

1. We trust you will see your way to *taking advantage of* our offer and await the favor of an early reply.

相信貴方會設法利用本公司的提案，敬待早日回信。

2. From our own *observations* and the *experiences* in the past, we believe you are the right people to represent us *in this line*, and should like to offer you the agency if you are at all interested, and we should welcome your *views*.

從過去的觀察和經驗，本公司相信貴方正是我方這種產品最佳代理商，若貴方有興趣，本公司願提供代理權，敬祈來函告知。

c) 接受代理權的提議（ Acceptance of Agency Offer ）

1. We have received your letter offering to act as your agent in our market. After careful consideration of *the contents of your offer*, we are ready to enter into the business which you propose.

   來函提議本公司爲此地市場代理商已收到。經愼重考慮該提案內容後，本公司準備與貴方締結此商務。

2. We thank you for your letter of June 19 appointing us your *sole agents* for Taiwan, and have pleasure in confirming our agreement to the conditions and terms *set forth* therein.

   感謝貴方6月19日來函，委任本公司爲台灣獨家代理商，並樂於確認對文中陳述的條件之認可。

3. We appreciate the confidence you show in us by offering us an agent for your products. The market conditions here are now rather active and *tend to welcome such quality goods* as yours, so we are sure there may be *bright prospects* for the advance of your market to this region. As this is the case, we are ready to meet your wishes to our mutual advantages and interests.

   感激貴方對本公司的信任，提議我方爲貴方產品的代理商。本地市場目前相當活躍，對像貴方這樣品質優良的貨品很歡迎，所以我方確信，貴方在本地拓展市場會有光明的遠景。有鑑於此，本公司準備順應貴方的願望，以增進相互的利益。

4. Thank you very much for your letter of March 1st informing us of your wish to *represent you* in our region, which we are ready to accept. We have some 20 *years' business background* here and want to help you in any way we can. Please *feel free to* write us about any problem which our experience might help you to solve.

非常感謝貴方3月1日的來函，告知有意以本公司為此地代理商，我方準備接受。本公司在此地有二十年的商務經歷，願盡力幫助貴方。任何問題只要以我方的經驗，可以幫貴方解決的，請儘管寫信告知。

5. We thank you for your letter of April 1 offering us the agency for your cameras in Brazil and appreciate *the confidence you have placed in us*.

感謝貴方4月1日來函，提供本公司在巴西照相機的代理權，並感激貴方對本公司的信賴。

6. We *endorse* your views as to the possibilities of the market, and believe that though sales for the first few months may be low, the final results will *justify* the establishment of the agency.

本公司贊同貴方對市場可能性之意見，相信雖然前幾個月的銷售額可能很低，但是最終的結果會證明代理權的成立是正確的。

7. We accept your offer *on the terms stated* and await your instructions.

在指定的條件下，本公司接受貴方的提議，並敬待貴方指示。

d) 對代理商的警告（ Warning to Agent ）

1. We note with surprise that your statement of expenses for the past month is ***unusually high***.

   注意到貴方上個月支出清單異常地高，本公司甚感驚訝。

2. Unless you can ***cut your expenses***, we shall be compelled to refuse further business. We trust that you will make every effort to ***cooperate with*** us ***in*** keeping expenses as low as possible.

   除非貴方能減少支出，本公司將被迫婉拒進一步的交易。相信貴方會盡力與本公司合作，使支出儘可能減低。

3. We note with regret that your sales for the past few months ***show a sharp decrease***, and while we admit that there may be a very good reason for this unsatisfactory state of affairs, we must ask you to ***submit detailed reports*** regularly.

   注意到貴方前幾個月的銷售額顯著減少，甚感遺憾。對這令人不滿意的事件，在承認其或許有很好的理由同時本公司必須要求貴方，定期提出詳細的報告。

4. A closer investigation has revealed that the sharp decline in the ***sales from your territory*** has counteracted the upward trend ***apparent elsewhere***.

   詳細的調查顯示，貴地市場銷售額迅速的下降，已經抵消了其他地方銷售明顯的增加趨勢。

   ➡ counteract〔͵kaʊntə'ækt〕*v*. 抵消；反動

5. We are confident that your *sales returns* will *prove the value* of cooperative effort.

相信貴方的銷售的收益，會證明合作努力的價值。

➡ return〔rɪ'tɜn〕*n.*(*pl.*) 報告書；收益

6. We regret to hear your opinion of our efforts during the last few months. You have failed to realize that the fall in our sales is *a direct result of your failure to cooperate with us*.

得知貴方對本公司前幾個月的努力之意見，深感遺憾。貴方未能了解銷售額的下降，乃貴方未能與我方合作的直接結果。

7. On examining the *monthly returns* submitted by you, we note that in the case of Contract 27 for September you have cut prices 10 percent. We have no doubt that you acted with the best of intentions, but you have totally *failed to* realize that such a reduction entirely *absorbs* the very small *margin of profit* on which *the running* of this business is based.

一檢查貴方提出的每月報告書，本公司就注意到，在9月第27號契約一案，貴方已減價百分之十。無疑地，貴方這麼做是基於好意，但是卻完全不了解這種降價完全吸收了在此交易中立足的極少利潤。

8. Further, we are very *averse to* your allowing special discounts as *this practice* is likely to give rise to awkward precedents.

再者，本公司非常反對貴方容許特殊的折扣，因為這麼做很可能導致棘手的先例。

9. As you have already ***committed yourselves***, however, we must stand by your arrangements, but we insist that in future you do not take such steps ***on your own initiative***.

　　既然貴方已經做了擔保，無論如何，本公司必須支持您的措施，但是卻堅持，今後貴方不可獨斷地採取此種行動。

　➡ commit〔kə′mɪt〕 *v*. 擔保；使自己負責任或受約束
　➡ initiative〔ɪ′nɪʃɪ,etɪv〕 *n*. 率先；主動

10. It is possible that ***awkward precedents*** may be set up, rendering return to the normal price difficult, if not impracticable. As this is the case, we would like to warn you against a cut in the ***prices named***, without consulting us, even if it is deemed necessary.

　　若非不能實行，可能建立起棘手的先例，使得回復正常價格變得困難。有鑑於此，本公司想警告貴方，即使認為必要，未與本公司商議不可降低指定價格。

e) 難以接受提出的代理權條件（ Proposed Agency Terms Unacceptable ）

1. For this reason, we cannot accept your agent.

　　為此理由，本公司不能答應做貴方的代理商。

2. They will not accept your agency on these terms.

　　在這些條件下，他們不會接受貴方的代理權。

3. We regret that we are *not in a position* to deal in your goods *on our account*, and we feel it just as difficult to accept your offer of agency on the proposed terms.

對於不能自行處理貴方的貨品，本公司深感遺憾，並認爲以所提出的條件，來接受貴方提供的代理權是很困難的。

4. We are grateful for your letter of March 10 offering us the *agency for your merchandise*, but regret to state that it is only as *sole agent* that we could accept your offer.

感謝3月10日來函，提供本公司貴方商品的代理權，但是很抱歉，只有當獨家代理商，本公司才可能接受貴方的提議。

5. In all probability you have not recognized that local conditions here render the proposed sales system almost *unworkable*.

很可能貴方並沒有體認到，本地的情況使得所提議的銷售制度幾乎不可行。

6. We fear that the volume of business would not be sufficient to justify the appointment of more than one agent, and are sure that a centralized scheme of *marketing* would be *productive of* the best results.

恐怕交易量不足以證明指派一家以上的代理店是正確的，我方確信集中銷售計畫會產生最好的成果。

7. We trust that you will now recognize advantages likely to result from our suggestions, and we

相信貴方現在會體認到由於我方建議可能會產生的利益，本公司可以

assure you that our wide experience and *valuable connections* should enable us to introduce your merchandise successfully into this country.

確保，以我方廣泛的經驗和寶貴的關係，將能把貴商品成功地介紹到本國。

8. Thank you very much for your kind offer to grant us an agency for your merchandise. In view of the local market conditions, however, should you *grant us a free hand* in minor matters, we would willingly accept your offer.

非常感謝貴方好意的提議，答應本公司貴商品的代理權。然而，鑑於本地市場的情況，若蒙答應細微末節由我方自由處理，則願接受貴方提議。

9. Should you be prepared to *leave* your price list *more or less to our discretion*, we would be ready to do our utmost to further your interests.

若貴方準備讓本公司多多少少自行處理價目表，本公司願盡力增進貴方的利益。

➡ discretion〔dɪ'skrɛʃən〕*n*. 行動的自由

B. 委託銷售 (Consignment Sales)

a) 提供委託銷售 (Offer of Consignment Sales)

1. Greetings: we are indebted to Messrs. John Smith & Co. in Boston *for your name*. They in-

敬啟者：感謝波士頓的約翰・史密斯公司提供貴方名字。據通知本商

form us that your trade and *con-nections in our line of business* are of the best and may we ask you if you would *be disposed to* work with us *on a consignment basis*?

務範圍內貴方的交易和關係是最好的。請問貴方是否有意和本公司以委託關係一起合作？

2. Please sell these consignments at the best possible price *for our account*.

請爲本公司的利益，以可能的最高價格銷售此委託品。

3. Kindly do the best you can with the goods as this is a new *venture for us*, which, if successful, we hope to repeat from time to time.

由於本產品對本公司是一種新的冒險，請盡力推銷。如果成功，我方希望往後時常重覆。

4. If you can *place this shipment* satisfactorily, we shall be pleased to forward larger consignments.

若蒙滿意地出售此次船貨，本公司樂意運送更多委託品。

5. The shipment is intended to *try your market*. Please put the goods before your buyers and telex us what offers you get and if they are reasonable, we shall be pleased to consider them.

本次船貨用意是試探貴市場。請展示給貴方買主，並電告我方您所得到的出價，若合理則樂於考慮。

6. We shall be glad if you can find
   an outlet for these goods among
   your buyers.

   ➡ outlet〔ˊaʊtlɛt〕*n.* 銷路；市場

若能在貴方買主間，為
這批貨找到銷路，則感
幸甚。

7. Kindly sell the goods as quickly
   as possible, and this, *even if at
   a small sacrifice*, has to be
   done.

請儘快賣掉這批貨，即
使必須稍微虧本出售也
可行。

8. We should be willing to consider
   a *small concession,* should you
   find it necessary.

若貴方認為必要，本公
司願考慮稍微讓步。

9. We do not wish to limit you as
   to prices, but rely on your doing
   your best to *dispose of* this
   small consignment.

至於價格，並沒有限制
貴方的意思，但是期待
您盡全力推銷這批少量
的委託品。

10. *We are given to understand* that
    you are doing a large trade in
    textile fabrics and have connec-
    tions with some of the buyers
    of *our class of goods.* We should
    be very much obliged, therefore,
    to have you *deal in* our goods on
    a consignment basis.

聽說貴方在紡織品方面
從事大量交易，並和一
些本公司經銷產品的買
主有關係。因此，若貴
方能以委託關係經營本
公司貨品，則不勝感激。

11. We are favorably impressed by the suggestions you have made. It is possible, however, that local conditions may *preclude* any heavy dealings, and with this possibility in mind, we cannot do more than forward a small consignment of 500 razors to *gauge the tastes of our prospective customers*.

本公司深爲貴方的提議所打動，然而當地市場的情況可能排除大量交易，鑑於有此可能性，故只能運送五百支刮鬍刀少量的委託品，以估量可能客戶的口味。

➡ preclude〔prɪ'klud〕*v*. 排除；防礙
➡ gauge〔gedʒ〕*v*. 估量；測定

12. We trust that you will be as *successful with* our products as with those of your other exporters.

相信貴方銷售本公司產品，會像銷售其他出口商的產品一樣成功。

b） 受託者→委託者（ Consignee → Consignor ）

1. We should be pleased to take care of any consignments of goods suitable for this market which you may be *disposed to* send us.

本公司很樂於關照貴方願意寄送，且適合本地市場的委託品。

2. We shall be pleased to receive a trial consignment from you,

本公司樂於接到貴方的試賣委託品，相信成果

which we trust will result satisfactorily to all concerned, and
also lead to a *more extensive
and mutually profitable business*
between us.

能使所有相關者滿意，
也能導致雙方更廣泛且
相互得利的交易。

3. Upon the arrival of the goods,
   we will use our best endeavors
   to *bring them under the notice
   of the trade here* generally.

一俟貨物到達，本公司
會盡力使本地同行普遍
注意它們。

4. We now await the shipment and
   will write you further when we
   have had the opportunity of
   testing the market.

本公司正在等貨運到，
一有機會在市場試銷，
會再寫信給貴方。

5. We shall do all in our power to
   deserve your confidence and to
   ensure your satisfaction with the
   results obtained.

本公司將盡全力證明值
得貴方信賴，並可確保
貴方對得到的成果滿意。

6. We regret to say that we are
   not meeting with much success in
   regard to the goods last shipped,
   as the market here is now quite
   flat.

關於上次運來的貨物，
因為本地市場目前相當
蕭條，本公司並未獲得
很大的成功，深感遺憾。

> ➡ flat〔flæt〕*adj.*　蕭條的；不景氣的

7. The goods are still **on our hands**,
   and will probably not sell **at anything like the prices you have
   fixed for them.**

   ➡ anything = *any prices*

   貨物尙在庫存中，依貴
   方所訂的價格將可能賣
   不出去。

8. **The prices** are at present **ruling
   very low**, and we have considered
   it to your interest to **hold over**
   your consignments.

   ➡ rule〔rul〕*v.* （價格等）維持；保持某一程度
   ➡ **hold over** 延期；延續

   目前價格維持偏低，本
   公司認爲委託品延期對
   貴方有利。

9. The market is now in a flourish-
   ing condition, and we can easily
   dispose of another similar consignment if delivered at an early
   date.

   目前市場繁榮，如果早
   日運到，本公司能輕易
   地賣掉類似的委託品。

10. We enclose Account Sales for the
    past month and will **credit you
    with** the amount shown, on re-
    ceipt of your confirmation of
    our figures.

    兹附寄上個月的寄銷清
    單，一俟接獲貴方對此
    數目的確認書，即將該
    金額記入貴方的貸方。

11. We have sold your consignment
    and enclose Account Sales and
    sight draft for **net proceeds**,
    which you **will please find in order**.

    貴方的委託品業已賣出，
    兹附上寄銷清單，和淨
    收入的卽期滙票，望查
    核無誤。

12. You will see by the Account Sales, which we enclose, that we were fortunate enough to *dispose of* these goods just before the fall of prices in this market, and so obtained fully 4 percent more than it would be possible to obtain today.

從附寄的寄銷清單，貴方將看出本公司有幸剛好在市場價格降低之前賣出這些貨物，所以比今天可能獲得的利潤整整多了百分之四。

13. Enclosed is the Account Sales for your consignment per s.s. WINDSOR CASTLE, showing *a balance of* $1,000 *in your favor*, which we trust you will *find correct*.

茲附寄貴方經由溫莎堡貨輪運來的委託品的寄銷清單，顯示貴方有一千元餘額，望查核無誤。

14. We regret to say that the present *low prices ruling* in this market render it impossible to obtain anything like *your figures*.

本地市場目前維持低價，以貴方的價格不可能成交，深感抱歉。

15. Fortunately, we were able to *place your shipments* as per prices named and hope to send Account Sales *in our next*.

本公司很榮幸能依貴方提出的價格把貨物賣出，希望下封信寄給貴方寄銷清單。

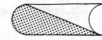 代 理・委 託 須 知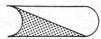

1. **connections** 〔kəˈnɛkʃənz〕 *n.* 客戶；業務關係

2. **market** 〔ˈmɑrkɪt〕 *v.* 出售；交易

3. **del credere commission（agreement）** 保證收取貨款傭金（合同）。del credere 是義大利語，意爲「買主付款保證」。通常代理商都是依照本店的價格進行交易，但此爲依照特別約定，向本店保證銷售對象付款的傭金。

4. **territory** 〔ˈtɛrə,torɪ〕 *n.* 商業範圍；銷路

5. **a balance in** *one's* **favor** ～受款的餘額

6. **to credit（debit）** *one* **with $1,000** 將一千元記入～的貸方（借方）

7. **give** *one* **free hand** 給予～處理上之完全自由

8. **be disposed to ～** 有意～

9. **be productive of** = *produce* 產生

10. **prejudice** *one's* **interest** 損害～的利益

11. **risk losses through bad debts** 因爲呆帳而冒虧損的危險

12. **on** *one's* **own initiative** 自行地

13. **be given to understand that ～** 聽說～

14. **be good（kind）enough to entertain** *one's* **wish for ～** 好意考慮某人對～的希望

15. **the trade** 同業者；同行

16. **trial consignment** 試賣的託售貨品

17. **market is flat** (*dull, bearish, bullish*)
    市場不景氣（不景氣，看跌，看漲）

18. **proceeds** [ˈprosidz] *n.(pl.)* (= *turnover*) 收入；收益

19. **sell off** 廉價出售；賣掉

20. **as** (*being*) **unsalable** 賣不出去
    as = *preposition*
    I consider it as (being) preferable.
    我認爲它比較好。

21. **deal in** 經營

22. **fall in with** = *agree to* (*with*) 同意

23. **feel free to** 不拘禮

24. **leave** (*something*) **to** *one's* **discretion** 使某人自行處理～

25. **for** *one's* **account** 以～的帳戶，以～價格
    on *one's* **account** 代理～，爲了～，自行
    The credit was opened in favor of A (exporter) *for account of* B (importer) up to the aggregate amount of US$5,000.
    以B（進口商）的帳戶開出以A（出口商）爲受款人，總額五千美元的信用狀。
    Your sales *on our account* have fallen considerably.
    貴方代理我方的銷售，有顯著的負成長。
    We are not in a position to deal with your goods *on our account*.
    本公司不能自行處理貴方的產品。

26. **The prices are ruling low (high).** 市場價格低迷（上揚）。

27. *one's* **class of goods** ～的經銷產品

28. **London and district** 倫敦及郊區

29. **prospective buyers** = *expected buyers* 可能的買主

30. **do business with** ～, *enter into business relations with* ～, *open an account with* ～ 和～進行交易

31. **prices named** 指定價格

32. **figure** 〔′fɪgɚ〕*n.* 計算；價格

33. **place** *one's* **shipment** 出售船貨

34. **in** *one's* **next** 以下一班船

35. **agent(s), seller(s), buyer(s)** → **agent, seller, buyer** 任何一方都非個人而是團體，所以要用複數。因此，即使用 our London agents，其意仍同於 our London agent。seller, buyer 也以機構為多，所以也有人用 sellers, buyers。同理可以了解，為什麼一家公司的代名詞，通常都用 they 來表示。

36. **banker** 〔′bæŋkɚ〕*n.* 交易銀行

37. **invoice amount（account, value）**
    發票的金額
    invoice volume
    發票的數量

代 理 ・ 委 託 模 範 書 信

A. 代理店關係

a）本店→代理商（ Principal → Agent ）

1

We have thoroughly considered the terms and conditions which you offered in your letter of February 15, and have decided to appoint you our *sole London Agent* . We are in agreement with your proposals except in a few minor points, and herewith give you in writing *the terms and conditions upon which we agree to work,* as follows:

We appoint you our sole London Agent for a period of twelve months from date, and agree to pay you commission on all orders received direct or indirect from London buyers. Being fully represented in *the provinces,* also in Wales, Scotland and Ireland, we must confine your area to London and *district,* by which a radius of 12 miles round London is to be understood. The commission we agree to pay you is 5 percent on the net amount of all *sales effected* by you on our behalf and executed by us. We also agree to allow the customers discount of 2.5 percent monthly on all ordinary prices, and special discounts to be arranged for special orders. Further we allow you 2.5 percent for *del credere*, as you have your own connections, and moreover, we wish to leave ourselves free to devote our energies to the manufacturing part of the business as much as possible. You will render us account of all sales made for us up to and including the 20th of each month, and remit us the amount of such sales, *less* discounts and commission on the 1st of the second month after; for instance, the *Account Sales* for January would be paid by your cheque on 1st March. We are also having some *circulars* prepared announcing your appointment as Agent , and will send these to you in the course of next week.

　　對於貴方2月15日來函提供的條件，已全盤考慮過，本公司決定委任貴方爲倫敦的獨家代理商。除了一些細節外，本公司同意貴方的提議，因此將我方同意經營的條件，條列如下：

　　玆委任貴方爲倫敦獨家代理商，卽日起爲期十二個月，並同意所有從倫敦買主直接或間接拿到的訂單，皆付傭金給貴方。因爲在各省以及在威爾斯、蘇格蘭、和愛爾蘭也皆有代理店，本公司必須將貴方的地區限定於倫敦及其周圍十二哩的區域。並同意付給貴方的傭金，是所有貴方代表我方銷售，而由我方履行的淨收益之百分之五。也同意每月給予客戶所有一般價格百分之二點五的折扣，對於特殊的訂單則有特別折扣。

再者，因為貴方有自己的交易關係，而且本公司希望儘可能致力於生產方面，對於貴方保證收取貨款，本公司同意給予貨款的百分之二點五。每個月貴方必須提出到二十日，當日包括在內的所有寄銷清單，並將這些銷售的金額，扣除折扣和傭金，在之後第二個月的第一天滙款過來。例如，1月的寄銷清單須在3月1日以支票付款。本公司尚有一些宣布委任貴方為代理商的通函，將於下週寄去。

➡ radius〔'redɪəs〕 *n.* 範圍；半徑
➡ *on one's behalf* = *on behalf of* ～ 代表～；為了～
➡ *del eredere* 保證收取貨款
➡ circular〔'sɜkjələ〕 *n.* 傳單；**商業通函**
➡ *in the course of* ～ 在～期間

b) 代理店→本店（ Agent → Principal ）

1

We regret that we are not in a position to deal in your goods on our account, and we must accordingly decline the offer of your weekly price lists, made on April 20. Your goods are quite unknown in this market and we very much doubt our ability to *place them* at your catalog prices. You will agree that in the circumstances *pricing can be no more than tentative*, and that with rigid quotations *the business would be quite unworkable*. As, however, we are unwilling to overlook a potential market, we would suggest that you allow us to handle your goods on a consignment basis, at *reserve prices* to be fixed by us in concert. We trust that our views will not discourage you; we are in fact inclined to think that a satisfactory trade could be built up in time. Provided, therefore, that you are prepared to *leave prices a great deal to our discretion*, we are ready to do our utmost to further your interests.

　　本公司因爲自身的緣故，不克經營貴方的貨品，深感遺憾，也因此必須拒絕貴方4月20日每週價目表的報價。貴方的貨品在本地市場幾乎無人知曉，故本公司很懷疑，是否能以貴方目錄上的價格訂購。貴方必然同意在此情況下，定價不能是暫時的，而報價不可通融則生意必然行不通。然而，因爲本公司不願忽視具有潛力的市場，故想建議貴方容本公司以委託銷售的關係，由雙方一起制訂最低價格，以銷售貴方貨品。相信本公司的觀點不致使貴方氣餒；實際上本公司認爲遲早會建立令人滿意的交易。因此，假若貴方準備大部分由我方自行設定價格，我方準備盡全力促進貴方利益。

➡ tentative〔'tɛntətɪv〕*adj.* 暫時的；試驗性的
➡ *in concert* 一起
➡ discretion〔dɪ'skrɛʃən〕*n.* 行動的自由

B. 委託銷售

a) 委託者→受託者（ Consignor → Consignee ）

1

We are favorably impressed by our friends' information concerning your firm, and are ready to *enter into the business* which you propose, as we have long been convinced that a good trade is to be done upon a consignment basis, provided a thoroughly reliable firm could be found willing to take up and push such a trade. Our friends inform us that you have a good connection in the flatware trade, and that you already import largely from this country, and acting entirely upon their advice we are sending you a consignment as a trial. The goods will be shipped by the s.s. Evergreen, sailing on April 10. We enclose herewith Consignment Note, and Bill of Lading will follow by next mail. We think your proposals with regard to Account Sales, viz., to render them monthly, quite satisfactory, and we will draw at three months for the amount of such sales, which will be rendered with your commission deducted. We are willing to allow you the extra 2.5 percent *for del credere*, as we of course could not

risk any losses through bad debts. Anything in reason
that we can do to assist you to create a demand for
our product in your market shall be done, and trusting
the present consignment will reach you safely, and
lead to a mutual profitable connection between us.

由於朋友供應的資料，我方對貴公司印象良好，並準備依您的提議，締結交易關係。因為我方長久以來深信，假使能夠發現一家全然值得信賴的公司，並願意從事及促進委託貿易，則好的交易應建立在委託銷售的基礎上。據我方朋友所言，貴方對於盤碟類的貿易，有良好的交易關係，且貴方已經大量從本國進口，本公司完全依從他們的建議，寄給貴方委託品以試銷。這批貨將由長榮號輪裝運，於 4 月 10 日出航。茲附寄託售單，提單下次奉寄。貴方建議每月提出寄銷清單，令本公司相當滿意，我方將開發銷售金額扣除備金後，三個月支付的滙票。對於保證收取貨款方面，本公司願給予貴方額外的百分之二點五，因為我方當然不能因呆帳而冒虧損的險。任何合理的事，只要我方辦得到，協助增加本公司產品在貴方市場上的需求量，一定照辦。相信這批委託品將安然送達，並導致雙方相互有利的關係。

➡ deduct〔dɪˈdʌkt〕*v*. 扣除

b) 受託者→委託者（ Consignee → Consignor ）

Our Account Sales for the March quarter is enclosed
with this letter and shows a balance of £2,100 in your
favor. If you will draw us for this amount at 60 days
we will accept the draft upon presentation. For your
information, *prices are ruling low* in our market making it gradually difficult to dispose of your consignments which are of rather high quality. This being the case, we presume some reduction in prices
seems inevitable if you wish to secure your position
in this locality. We are also prepared to accept a 2
percent cut in commission if you are prepared to make
an allround price cut. We look forward to your reply
and wish to assure you of increased effort *on your
behalf*.

　玆隨函附寄三月這一季的寄銷清單，顯示貴方受益的二千一百英鎊
的餘額。若蒙貴方開發等金額見票六十天支付的滙票，本公司將在提出
時立即承兌。本地市場價格持續低落，使得賣掉貴方的委託品越來越困
難，因該貨品質相當高。有鑑於此，若貴方想在本區佔有一席之地，本
公司認爲稍微降低價格是不可避免的。若貴方預備全盤降價，我方也準
備接受減少百分之二的傭金。期盼貴方回音，想向您保證會爲貴方多盡
些力量。

第11章
信託收據・保證書
Trust Receipt · Letter of Guarantee

1.信託收據　T/R (Trust Receipt)

　　進口商若未付清出口商開出的滙票，就無法拿到裝船文件，這是貿易的原則。但是，就進口商而言，當然希望在付款之前先得到貨品，待銷售後取得貨款，再付清滙票金額。這時進口商可以送交 **Trust Receipt**，簡稱 **T/R（信託收據）**，向銀行借提裝運文件。因為此時貨物抵押在銀行，貨主只要有同等的抵押，就可售貨，然後在到期日付清滙票，即可取回抵押。

　　就拿D/P（付款後交單據）遠期滙票來說，在期票到期日之前，無法領到裝運文件，所以必須先利用T/R借提裝運文件。若為即期滙票，進口商無資金付款時，雖然可以向融資銀行調度資金，但由於裝運文件

抵押在銀行，仍然提不到進口貨品，所以得向銀行提出T/R，借提裝運文件，以便取得貨物，換取需求金額，於期滿之日付清滙款。

這種T/R是始於美國的一種週轉手段，銀行藉此將**抵押品（col-lateral goods）**的所有權轉移到進口商手中。

```
┌─────────────────────────────────────┐
│     信 託 收 據 必 備 例 句          │
└─────────────────────────────────────┘
```

1. The draft is 60 d/s D/P, so we *tendered* a T/R to BANK OF TAIWAN, TAIPEI, and received the cargo, which you will please note.

因為滙票是見票後六十天付款的付款後交單據，所以本公司提出信託收據給台北的台灣銀行，並且收到了貨物，惠請注意。

2. The draft is D/P at 60 d/s, so we received the cargo *on a T/R* tendered to BANK OF TAIWAN, TAIPEI. The draft to be cleared on October 1, due date.

因為滙票是見票後六十天付款的付款後交單據，所以本公司提給台北台灣銀行信託收據，並已收到該批貨物。本滙票預定在支付日期10月1日結算。

3. The importer is able to obtain the B/L before the *clearance* of his Usance D/P draft by the production of a T/R to the bankers.

進口商能夠經由提出信託收據給交易銀行，而在付清遠期D/P滙票前，取得提單。

➡ Usance D/P draft 遠期付款後交單據滙票

4. A T/R is an expedient for the importer on whom a Usance D/P was drawn to obtain his cargo before the bill *falls due*.

信託收據是讓進口商於遠期D/P滙票到期前，取得貨物的權宜之計。

➡ expedient〔ɪk'spidɪənt〕*n*. 權宜之計

5. The T/R system originally developed in the US is now available on the international scale but in the Latin American nations.

信託收據制度最初在美國發展，現在除了拉丁美洲國家之外，在國際間已大規模採用。

6. The T/R system permits the importer to dispose of the *collateral goods* before the clearance of his Usance D/P draft, so this privilege is granted to the trader deemed most reliable and trustworthy.

信託收據制度允許進口商，在付清遠期D/P滙票之前，可以處理抵押貨品，因此只有被認為最可靠和值得信賴的貿易商，才被允許此項特權。

2.保證書 Letter of Guarantee

L/G（保證書）和T/R一樣，是向銀行或船公司提出的保證書。需要提呈L/G的情況，說明如下：

1. 貨物已經抵達進口地而裝運文件卻尚未送達時，貨主可聯合銀行向船公司提出**保證書**（ **Letter of Guarantee → L/G** ），以取得貨

品。這時 L/G 就是 B/L 的代替品。此外，L/G 必須以在一定期限內繳交裝運文件給船公司為條件，一旦裝運文件寄達銀行，就必須以 T/R 向銀行借提裝運文件，再以裝運文件換回 L/G。總之，L/G 終究要換成 T/R，所以和 T/R 一樣具有處理**抵押品**（ collateral goods ）的效力，相當於 B/L 到達前的 T/R。

2. 在出口地押滙銀行進行押滙，由於裝運文件**不齊**（ irregularities ），銀行拒絕押滙時，要向銀行提出 L/G，請求押滙。

3. foul B/L（瑕疵提單）要換成 clean B/L（清潔提單）時，也要向船公司提出 L/G，否則銀行可以瑕疵提單為由，拒絕押滙。

4. 出口商在完成裝船後二十一天，才向押滙銀行提呈 B/L 時，銀行可以用 stale B/L（過期提單）為由拒絕押滙，這時出口商也必須向銀行提出 L/G，請求押滙。

【說明】　a）新信用狀統一條例規定，裝船後二十一天以上的 B/L，銀行得以拒絕押滙。

　　　　b）新信用狀統一條例規定，L/G 只在出口商和押滙銀行之間持有效力，在其他方面並不具有強制力。

　　　　c）以上 2、4 的押滙，稱為 L/G 押滙。

　　　　d）L/G 原本稱為 Letter of Indemnity（ L/I，賠償保證書），最近才普遍被稱作 L/G。

保 證 書 必 備 例 句

1. Your shipment has arrived, but the B/L unreached, so we have received the cargo **on an L/G**.

   貴方的船貨已到,但提單未到,所以本公司以保證書收取貨物。

2. The bankers refused to negotiate the draft due to **irregularities in the documents**, but the exporter attained the purpose by presentation of an L/G to the bankers.

   銀行以裝運文件不齊為由,拒絕押滙,但該出口商以提出保證書給銀行而達到目的。

3. A **foul B/L** can be made a **clean B/L** upon production of an L/G, so caution must be taken even against a clean B/L.

   瑕疵提單可經由保證書而變成清潔提單。所以,甚至是清潔提單也必須加以小心謹慎。

4. The bankers may reject the B/L when presented later than 21 days after the issuance thereof.

   在發布二十一天以後才提出的提單,銀行可以拒受。

5. Provision No. 8 of the Revised Uniform Customs & Practice for Documentary Credits rules that the guarantee or reserve in respect of **any irregularities in the documents** concerns only the relations between the negotiation bank and the beneficiary.

   「修訂跟單信用狀統一慣例」第八號條款規定,有關文件不齊的保證或保留,只限於押滙銀行和受益人之間的關係。

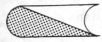信託收據・保證書須知

1. **tender, presentation, production** 提出

2. **clear the bill** 付清支票

3. **clearance** 〔'klɪrəns〕*n*. 結關證書，出〔入〕港執照，付清

4. **collateral goods** 抵押品

5. **Revised Uniform Customs & Practice for Documentary Credits** 1974年修訂的有關跟單信用狀統一慣例。於 1974年12月的 ICC（International Chamber of Commerce, 國際商會）會員大會中通過。1975年10月1日實施。這項修訂在貿易的發展狀況及貨櫃運輸上，可說是劃時代的修正。世界各國遵從 ICC的勸告，照章實施的國家達百分之九十。

信 託 收 據 ・ 保 證 書 模 範 書 信

A. 信託收據（Trust Receipt, T/R）

1

We are pleased to inform you that your shipment of August 10 —— KGK's 10 metric tons of CEMENT Grade A packed in 200/50 kg paperbags —— has arrived in Keelung on board the s.s. "President Wilson". The draft, however, is 60 d/s D/P and we have **tendered a T/R to** the First Commercial Bank, Keelung and received the cargo, which you will please note.

貴方8月10日的船貨—— KGK十公噸A級水泥，以每袋五十公斤包裝共兩百紙袋——已到達基隆，在威爾遜總統號船上，特函奉告。然而滙票是見票後六十天付款的付款後交單據，本公司已提出信託收據給基隆的第一商業銀行，以收取貨物，惠請注意。

➡ metric〔'mɛtrɪk〕*adj.* 米突制的；公尺的（ metric ton " 公噸 "）
➡ cement〔sə'mɛnt〕*n.* 水泥

B. 保證書（ Letter of Guarantee , L/G ）

2

For your information, your shipment of our July 30th order No. 205 for 50 units of SINGER SEW-ING MACHINES fully automatic Model D—50 arrived in Kaohsiung yesterday, but the B/L has not yet reached, so we have received the cargo **on an L/G**.

特予通知，本公司7月30日第205號訂單，所要的五十台D—50型全自動勝家縫紉機船貨，在昨天抵達高雄，但提單尚未到，所以我方以保證書收取貨物。

第12章
訴怨・索賠
Complaints & Claims

　　貿易上的**索賠**（claim），乃進口商對於因貨品損傷、短裝、品質不良、延遲交貨、與樣品不符等所引起的損失，要求賠償，亦即行使要求權。這類事件經常由於當事者之間的爭端（dispute），終至對簿公堂。當然，若非嚴重損失，只是輕微的 trouble 或 breakdown（損壞），最好還是能夠和平解決（amicable settlement）。

　　在與對方訴怨以求取賠償時，務必要嚴正、清楚地敍述事實。千萬避免使用指責對方「蓄意造成此損失」的語句。不能諒解對方的語句及態度，只有負面效果罷了（事實上經常是因不可抗力因素引起的）。根據事實，清楚、簡潔、有力的寫法才是正確的解決之道。

收到訴怨與索賠函的一方，在回覆時絕對不可使用「看到貴方來信甚爲驚訝」「我們無法了解這種情況」等語句。應該誠心聽取對方的陳訴，並表示「定儘速調查此事」「盡全力照您的指示辦理」。若對方的說法失當，可以要求他們鄭重、清楚的說明。務必在繼續往來的前提之下，爲對方的立場設想。

訴 怨 · 索 賠 必 備 例 句

A. 進口商→出口商（Importer → Exporter）

1. We are sorry to *have to inform* you that....

   必須告知貴方…，甚感遺憾。

2. We have duly received the goods of your shipment, but *unfortunately*....

   本公司已按時收到貴方船貨，然不幸…。

3. It is with great regret that we *have to inform* you that your last delivery proved three packages short of the invoiced volume.

   必須告知貴方上次送的貨，證實較發票所列數量不足三包，至感遺憾。

4. Thank you for your letter dated April 16 *advising* us of the shipment of our order ～. On checking the goods received, we found that....

   貴方4月16日來函，告知本公司訂貨～的船運，至爲感激。檢驗收到的貨物時，我方發現…。

5. We have received your letter dated April 15 and thank you for
   sending us a consignment of our
   order. ***Unfortunately***, ***however***,
   ....

   本公司已收到貴方 4 月
   15 日的信函，感謝您寄
   來我方訂購的寄售品。
   然而不幸…。

   ➡ consignment〔kən′saɪnmənt〕*n.* 委託 (貨) 物；寄售品

6. We have received the goods of
   your shipment, but they are not
   in any way ***up to our sample***.

   本公司已收到貴方發運
   的貨品，然而它們與我
   方的樣品全然不符。

7. The delay has caused us great inconvenience, ***necessitating*** many
   awkward explanations to our customers : we trust that there will
   be no repetition of the trouble.

   該延誤使我方必須對客
   戶作許多尷尬的解釋，
   造成很大的不便：相信
   將不會再有此麻煩才是。

   ➡ necessitate〔nə′sɛsə,tet〕*v.* 需要

8. An examination of the goods of
   your last delivery proved that
   they are far ***below standard***. We
   estimate, in fact, that they will
   not fetch more than 80 percent
   of the sum charged for them, and
   we consider ourselves ***entitled***
   to an allowance for the loss we
   must suffer.

   檢視貴方上次遞送的貨
   物，證實其遠在標準之
   下。本公司估計事實上
   它們賣不到其索價金
   額的百分之八十，我方
   認為有權要求得到所蒙
   受損失的津貼。

   ➡ fetch〔fɛtʃ〕*vt.* 售得

9. Samples have been most *mislead-ing*, and in some cases, we are almost convinced that goods not ordered have been forwarded by mistake.

樣品非常令人不解，以某些情況看來，我方幾乎確信，非我方訂購的貨品也誤送來了。

➡ forward〔'fɔrwəd〕*vt.* 運送；轉遞

10. The inferiority of the packing is likely to *prejudice* prospective customers, who are apt to judge by appearances. We trust that you will now give your goods *the packing they deserve*.

劣等的包裝可能使易由外表來判斷的可能客戶有壞印象。相信貴方會給您的貨物應有的包裝。

➡ prejudice〔'prɛdʒədɪs〕*vt.* 使存偏見
➡ prospective〔prə'spɛktɪv〕*adj.* 有希望的

11. We regret to *bring to your notice* certain grave irregularities in connection with our order No. 600 of May 15.

我方5月15日第600號訂單有某些嚴重的不符情事，惠請注意。

12. We hope to hear from you by return that the consignment is *on its way*.

希望接到信後，立刻回覆本公司，委託貨品已送出。

13. We urged on you *the importance of the time factor*.

促請貴方注意時間因素的重要性。

14. Although the quality of **the goods** is not up to that of our usual lines, we are prepared to accept them if you will reduce the price, say, **by** 10 **percent**.

雖然這批貨物的品質，未達本公司一般貨物的標準，如蒙降低百分之十的價格，我方準備接受。

15. Unfortunately, we find you have sent us **the wrong goods**.

不幸，本公司發現貴方送錯貨物。

進口商→出口商的結尾語

1. We must accordingly ask you to **examine** very carefully the pieces despatched and inform us of the results of your examination.

因此，本公司得請求貴方審慎檢驗寄去的樣品，並告知檢驗結果。

2. Please let us know what you can do to help us.

懇請告知貴方所能協助我方之事。

3. We shall expect to hear from you immediately as to what you **intend to** do in this instance.

本公司期待即刻接獲貴方來函，告知關於您對此事的打算。

4. We shall be glad if you will **look into** the matter and advise us of the results.

如蒙貴方調查該問題，並告知結果，本公司將至感幸甚。

5. **An explanation of this delay will be appreciated**.

若蒙對此次延誤來函說明，將不勝感激。

B. 出口商→進口商 (Exporter → Importer)

1. Upon receipt of your letter, pointing to **faults in** our products, we immediately passed your complaints on to the factory for close checkup.

一接獲貴方指陳本公司產品有瑕疵的來函，我方立即將您的訴怨轉告工廠，要求做周詳的檢查。

2. As soon as we received your letter of March 16, we **got in touch with** the packers and asked them to **look into** the matter.

本公司一接獲貴方3月16日來函，就與包裝業者聯絡，請求他們調查該問題。

3. **Disciplinary action** has been taken against those **responsible for** the error and a repetition of the trouble is most unlikely.

過失的責任者已受到懲戒處分，不可能會再發生這種麻煩。

→ disciplinary〔'dɪsəplɪn,ɛrɪ〕*adj.* 懲戒的

4. We are sorry to have your complaint respecting the goods we sent you on May 6, but at the same time **we can assure you** that they were **in perfect order** when they left here, and damage has, therefore, occurred **during transit**.

獲悉貴方對於本公司在5月6日所送交貨物的訴怨，我方甚感抱歉。同時可向您保證，貨物在離開此地時全然無損，因此破損是在運送途中發生的。

→ transit〔'trænsɪt,-zɪt〕*n.* 運送；搬運

5. As we have hopes of *getting the trouble cleared up* in the very near future, we would ask you to do *nothing final* yet.

可望於不久的將來解決
麻煩，故懇求貴方尚勿
做最後的處置。

出口商 → 進口商的結尾語

1. Unfortunately you have suffered considerable inconvenience, and *for the present we can only ask you to accept our apologies*.

不幸貴方蒙受了相當大
的不便，現今，本公司
只能請求您接受我方的
道歉。

2. We greatly regret all these irregularities and should welcome an opportunity to *set things right* as early as possible.

對這些不合規格的貨品
深感遺憾，並歡迎有儘
早改善的機會。

3. We regret the loss you must suffer and are anxious to do all we can to *mitigate* it.

➡ mitigate〔'mɪtə,get〕 *vt.* 使減輕

貴方所蒙受的損失，本
公司甚感遺憾，並渴望
盡一切所能來減輕之。

4. We must *ask you to accept our apologies* for the inconvenience you have been caused, and grant us further opportunities to *regain your confidence*.

造成貴方不便，請接受
本公司致歉，並允許我
方有進一步重獲您信賴
的機會。

5. We should be grateful if you would still ***honor us with your confidence***.

如蒙貴方繼續惠予信賴，本公司將不勝感激。

6. We apologize sincerely for the trouble caused you and will ***take all possible steps to*** ensure that such a mistake will not be made again.

本公司由衷地為引起貴方的麻煩致歉，並將採取一切可能措施，確保如此的錯誤永不再犯。

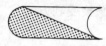 訴 怨 · 索 賠 須 知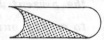

1. **have to** 經常用於壞消息的通知上。
   We are sorry to **have to** inform you of the damage caused to your shipment of our order during the transit from Singapore to London.

   很抱歉通知貴方，我方訂購貨品在從新加坡到倫敦的運送途中遭致損失。

2. 以下的說法，請儘量避免使用。
   a) We are astonished at your complaint, as *no other customers have ever found faults in our material.* → 態度硬直
   b) The delay was *not our fault.* → 過份幼稚
   c) As the mistake was made *on your part*, we are not held responsible for the mishap. → 火爆

   應改正如下：
   a) Upon receipt of your letter pointing to faults in our products, we immediately ***passed your complaints on to the factory for close checkup into the mishap***. We are very sorry for this incident, and....

在收到貴方指摘我方產品缺點的同時，我方立刻將貴方的訴怨轉告工廠，以便調查這不幸事件。我方非常抱歉，… 。

b) We are extremely sorry about this delay, which you will realize was **due to the circumstances beyond our control**.

我方對這次的延遲感到極其抱歉，希望貴方將了解，這是在我方無法控制的情況下發生的。

c) We consider it **not exactly reasonable to press the responsibility upon us because**, we presume, you are apparently involved in the mishap.

我方認為您把責任推卸給我方並不合理，因為本公司認為貴方顯然地與這不幸事件有關。

3. **defective goods** 有瑕疵的貨物
   export rejects 外銷不合格產品
   rejected goods 退貨

訴 怨・索 賠 模 範 書 信

A. 進口商 → 出口商（Importer → Exporter）

1

It is with regret and a certain amount of surprise that we find you have not yet delivered the goods ordered two months ago. As the **undertaking** of your representative to effect prompt delivery was an important factor in bringing us to place this order with you, we must insist on *standing by* his statement. The goods are required for shipment and must be with us in four days ; should you fail in your obligations, we should be compelled to cancel the order.

發現貴方尚未遞送兩個月前所訂購之貨物，本公司甚覺遺憾，也感到些許驚訝。因爲貴方代表保證即期交貨，是使我方向您訂購的重要因素，我方堅持貴方遵守其聲明。請裝運貨物，並於四天內送交本公司；萬一貴方無法履行義務，我方將被迫取消訂單。

➡ undertaking 〔͵ʌndə'tekɪŋ〕 *n*. 保證
➡ effect 〔ə'fɛkt,ɪ-,-ɛ-〕 *vt*. 實現

2

Your shipment of our order arrived in Kaohsiung yesterday. While *checking* the goods, we found that the three pieces of 100 machines we ordered had been *damaged in part*. Could you *replace* them with the complete ones? We are in urgent need of them, and look forward to your prompt reply.

　　本公司訂購的船貨於昨日抵達高雄。檢視貨物時，我方發現所訂購的一百台機器中，有三台部分受損。可否請您用完好的機器更換呢？本公司對此有急需，期望您早日回覆。

B. 出口商→進口商（ Exporter → Importer ）

1

We are very sorry to hear that the goods reached you in an unsatisfactory condition. The trouble might have been caused by the mispacking *at our end* or the careless handling *in transit*. Anyway, *we are ready to replace* the broken pieces with the new ones, and won't you take the trouble of sending the damaged goods back to us, carriage forward? Very sorry again for the trouble and inconvenience caused you.

　　聽說到達貴方的貨物受損，本公司甚感抱歉。麻煩可能起因於我方的錯誤包裝，或運送途中的粗心處理。然而，我方準備用新的更換損毀部分，可否請您費神將受損的貨物寄回，運費由收件人負擔呢？再次為導致貴方的麻煩與不便深深致歉。

　　➡ carriage forward 〔英〕運費由收件人負擔

> **2**
>
> We have received your letter of September 4 and immediately *telexed you*, as per copy enclosed, stating that the goods were despatched on the 1st, which we confirm.

本公司已接獲貴方九月四日的來函,並立即以電傳通知貴方,照附寄的副本所示,聲明我方確實在一日時發送貨物。

➡ telex〔ˈtɛlɪks〕*vt.* 拍發商務交換電報

第13章
抗議函

Protests

　　抗議函與前一章的訴怨、索賠大致相同，而性質更強硬，語氣也更重。在商業交易中，經常因為不履行契約、停止出貨、長期拒付、不支付滙款、重大失誤或嚴重損傷而引起買賣當事人之間的爭論。能夠處理這種重大事態的信函，非抗議函莫屬，以表示我方**堅決**（ firm ）的態度。文章必須清晰、嚴謹，且文體須是**強力有效**（ effective and powerful ）的。

抗 議 函 必 備 例 句

A. 進口商→出口商（ Importer → Exporter ）

1. *We must draw your attention to ...*　　　　本公司必須請您注意…。

2. We must **strongly protest against**
the great delay of our consignment in its arrival here.

我方強烈抗議寄售品送
抵此地時延誤過久。

3. Your shipments of our order have
reached us, but to our surprise,
they are **not in any way up to
the sample** you sent us.

本公司訂購的船貨已送
達，但至爲驚訝的是，
它們根本與寄來的樣品
不合。

4. You are **requested** to act
promptly.

敬請貴方迅速執行。

5. We cannot **endure** to continue our
negotiations any longer and would
like this to be **our last writing
to you.**

本公司無法再忍受繼續
交涉下去，希望這是最
後一次寫信給貴方。

6. We are compelled to express our
strong disapproval of the highly
unsatisfactory way in which you
handled our last order.

對貴方處理本公司上回
訂單，所採用之令人極
爲不滿的方式，我方不
得不表達強烈的反對。

B. 出口商→進口商（ Exporter → Importer ）

1. We very much regret the necessity of reminding you once again
of your failure in the remittance
of your **long-overdue** account.

必須再次提醒貴方，您
過期已久的帳款尚未滙
來，本公司甚感遺憾。

2. There was a delay in the shipment due to *the breakdown of*
some machines, which held up
production for one week, for
which we deeply apologize.

由於一些機器故障，而
停止生產一週，致船貨
方面有所延誤，本公司
對此深表歉意。

➡ breakdown〔'brek,daʊn〕 *n.* 故障；損壞
➡ hold up 使停滯；停止

3. Please *feel it easy* as the goods
are already *on their way* and the
documents were duly handed to
the bank.

貨物已在運送途中，而
且文件也按時交給銀行，
敬請放心。

4. Your order was unfortunately
overlooked *in the pressure of*
business, but we assure you that
every effort will be made in future to guarantee delivery *in ac-*
cordance with your requirements.

貴方的訂單不幸因業務
繁忙而忽略了，但本公
司向您保證，今後會盡
一切努力，以保根據您
的要求交貨。

出口商→進口商的結尾語

1. We request you to settle the
long-overdue account without further delay, otherwise you may
expose yourselves to unpleasant
consequences.

懇請貴方立即解決過期
已久的帳款，否則將會
招致很不愉快的後果。

2. It was with great regret that we read your final remarks, and we sincerely hope *you will not consider it necessary to* take such a drastic step.

讀到貴方最後的意見，甚感遺憾，並衷心的希望，您不會認爲必須採取如此激烈的措施。

➡ drastic〔ˊdræstɪk〕*adj.* 激烈的

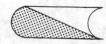 抗 議 函 須 知

請背下以下片語

1. **feel（it）easy** 覺得安心

2. **in the pressure of business** 在業務繁忙中

3. **breakdown of～** ～的故障

4. **as requested** 依所請，按照要求

抗 議 函 模 範 書 信

A. 進口商→出口商（ Importer → Exporter ）

1

We must *protest strongly against* the delay in the delivery of our order. We have so far phoned and wired you, but still *we are without the goods*. This is

causing us the greatest inconvenience, and we are los-
ing trade through it every day. We must really ask you
to let us have the goods immediately or return our
order. We find it most unreasonable that you should
treat an old customer in this way.

本公司不得不強烈抗議訂貨遞送的延誤。迄今我方已打過電話、拍過電報給您，卻依然收不到貨品。這造成本公司最大的不便，每天因而喪失交易機會。我方確實必須要求您即刻出貨，或者退還訂單。本公司認為貴方這樣對待老客戶，非常不合理。

➡ wire〔waɪr〕*v.* 向…拍電報

2

We regret to remind you that no advices have been
received from you as to the execution of our special
order of May 2 for soap and soap-powder. As ***the
undertaking of your representative to effect prompt
delivery*** caused us to ***decide in your favor***, and reject more favorable ***tenders from elsewhere***, we
must insist on your ***standing by*** your statement. You
will remember that we stressed the importance of
an early delivery, and you will understand that your
delay in the circumstances gives us a right to ***sue***

> *for damages.* We are unwilling to exercise this right,
> however, and are prepared to wait for the goods till
> May 17, on which date their shipment to our custom-
> ers is due. We trust that you will make every effort
> to prevent our taking a step which would be *as un-*
> *welcome to us as to you.*

很遺憾提醒貴方，本公司5月2日特別訂購的肥皂和肥皂粉，尚未接獲履行通知。因爲貴方代表保證即期交貨，本公司遂決定向貴公司訂購，而拒絕別處更有利的投標，所以我方堅持貴方遵守聲明。您記得本公司曾強調及早交貨的重要性，也了解在這種情況下的延誤，我方有權提出損害賠償的告訴。然而，本公司不願運用這項權利，而準備等貨到5月17日，即貨品預定送達我方客戶的日子。相信貴方會盡一切努力，避免我方採取對彼此都不愉快的措施。

➡ sue〔su〕*v.* 起訴；提出控告 (*sue for damages* 提出損害賠償的告訴)

B. 出口商→進口商 (Exporter → Importer)

1

> It is with deep regret that we must write over and
> over again to ask for the remittance of your three-
> months-overdue account on our books. Up to date, we
> have not even received *the courtesy of your reply.*
> Therefore, we have regretfully reached the conclusion

that there is left only the *final resort to legal meas-ures*, and we have placed your case in the hands of the attorney.

對於必須一再寫信，請求貴方滙付過期三個月的書籍帳款，深表遺憾。迄今，本公司甚至未接獲您的回覆。因此，我方遺憾地達成結論，最後只有訴諸法律途徑，並將貴方的案例委託律師處置。

➜ attorney〔ə´tɜnɪ〕 *n.* 律師

2

All our attempts to induce you to *clear your indebt-edness to us* have been ignored, and we are quite un-able to understand why you have not even replied to our letters. We have shown reasonable patience and consideration, but we can‘do so no longer and must now reluctantly take steps to obtain payment at law.

對勸誘貴方清償積欠債務的一切嘗試，貴方均置之不理。而且甚至沒回信，令人著實感到不解。我方表現了合理的耐心與體恤，但是，卻無法再如此下去，現在不得不勉強採取法律措施，以取得欠款。

➜ indebtedness〔ɪn´dɛtɪdnɪs〕 *n.* 債務

第14章
道歉・婉拒函
Letters of Apology
& Regret

1.道歉函 Letters of Apology

　　與十二章、十三章中敍述的訴怨、索賠、抗議函相對的就是**道歉函**。致歉函件在社交上的應用也極頻繁，但本章談的僅限於貿易關係──進出口商之間的交易。若進口商的訴怨、抗議，錯誤確實在出口商時，誠懇地向對方敍述原因、境況是非常重要的。並要**承諾絕不重蹈覆轍**，希望今後繼續惠顧指教。較長的致歉函，除了在破題處致 apology 之外，最好於末尾再次 apologize。

道 歉 函 必 備 例 句

1. First of all, we would like to *tender our heartfelt apology for* ....

   首先對…致上衷心的歉意。

2. We offer you *a thousand pardons for* ....

   本公司對…感到萬分抱歉。

3. Please accept our deep apologies for....

   請接受本公司對…深深的歉意。

4. First, we must apológize sincerely for....

   首先必須對…誠摯地道歉。

5. May we ask you *indulgence* (leniency) with regard to...?

   關於…可以要求貴方寬容嗎?

   ➡ leniency〔ˈlinjənsɪ〕 *n*. 寬容;仁慈

6. Will you kindly accept our apology for ～?

   能否接受本公司對～的道歉?

7. We have *no words* how to apologize to you for....

   本公司對…不知該如何致歉。

8. We would again ask for your *leniency in this instance.*

   對於此事,再次要求貴方寬容。

9. Please accept our many apologies for the trouble caused〔to〕 you by *the clerical mistake at our end*.

由於本公司抄寫的錯誤，而爲貴方引起的麻煩，請接受我方道歉。

道歉函結尾語

1. We again apologize for *causing* you much inconvenience.

再次爲引起貴方諸多不便致歉。

2. Apologizing again for *causing* you inconvenience, but *soliciting continuance of* your patronage and favors,

再次爲引起貴方的不便致歉，但是懇求貴方繼續惠顧支持。

3. We would *defer* the expression of our apologies *to our interview*.

容會面時再申我方抱歉之忱。

4. As this is the case, please pardon us for causing you *much inconvenience* and we sincerely look forward to *further* business with you.

有鑑於此，請原諒本公司爲貴方引起許多不便，並誠摯地期待與貴方更進一步的交易。

5. We again apologize sincerely for the *trouble* caused〔to〕 you and will take all possible *steps* to ensure that such a mistake is not made again *in future*.

再次爲引起貴方的麻煩致上誠摯的歉意，並將採取所有可能的措施，以確保這種錯誤今後不會再犯。

6. We will *do all in our power* not
   to repeat such a failure *in
   future*.

   本公司將竭盡所能，今
   後不再犯同樣的失誤。

7. We would like to make every
   endeavor to prevent the *recurr-
   ence* of such a failure and would
   be glad to be favored with your
   further *commands*.

   本公司會竭盡所能以避
   免再犯同樣失誤，並且
   樂於有幸再為貴方效勞。

2.婉拒函　Letters of Regret

　　婉拒函（Letters of Regret）　被列為書信中最困難的一類。書寫
重點在不傷害對方的感情又不失禮節。破題不寫拒絕文句，應該先對其
來信敬表謝忱。然後表明不得不加以婉拒的理由，最後再次致意。如
「因為種種情況而無法遵行其意」「待情況好轉再為貴方效力」之類的。
這種**為對方著想**，委婉拒絕的技巧極為重要。總之，這是一種需要運用
靈活技巧的信函。

婉　拒　函　必　備　例　句

1. Thank you very much for your
   letter of May 15. To our *regret*,
   however,....

   非常感謝貴方5月15日
   來函。然而，…令本公
   司很遺憾。

2. We have received your letter of May 15, but are very *sorry* to tell you that....

貴方5月15日來函敬悉，但是非常抱歉必須告訴您…。

3. We deeply *appreciate* your kind- ness (courtesy, great efforts, *etc.*) but are sorry to have to advise you that....

深深感謝貴方的好意（恩惠，努力等），但是很抱歉必須通知貴方…。

4. To our deep regret, however, we are unable to *meet* your kind offer.

然而，本公司無法接受貴方好意的報價，深感遺憾。

5. Under such circumstances, we have *no choice but to* decline your order....

在這種情況下，本公司不得不婉拒貴方的訂單…。

6. We feel we must return your order, *with our apologies and best thanks*.

我方認為必須退還貴方的訂單，很抱歉並深深感謝貴方。

7. We wish you to *understand our position* of having to decline your offer.

希望貴方能諒解本公司必須婉拒報價的處境。

8. After *carefully considering* your offer, however, we have come to the conclusion that....

然而，在慎重考慮貴方的報價後，我方達成的結論是…

婉拒函的結尾語

1. We are really *sorry not to be helpful*, but hope that you will understand our position.

眞的很抱歉不能有所幫助，但是希望貴方會理解本公司的處境。

2. We regret our *inability to meet your offer* (requirements), but hope to be favored with your continued favors and attention.

很遺憾不能接受貴方的報價（要求），但是希望有幸蒙貴方繼續支持與關照。

3. *Please accept our apologies* not to be helpful to you.

因爲不能對貴方有所助益，請接受我方致歉。

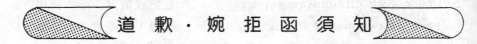

道 歉 · 婉 拒 函 須 知

1. inconveniences **caused**〔**to**〕you 的 to 可以省略。

2. 請記下下面的片語
   at our end 在我方
   at your end 在貴方
   the payment at our end 我方的付款
   the payment at your end 貴方的付款

3. **do all in** *one's* **power** 竭盡所能

4. 今後絕不再犯這種錯誤
   （exaggeration）→ We *assure you that we will never repeat such a failure in future.*
   （better）→ We will **do all in our power not to repeat such a failure in future.**

5. **in future** 今後（與迄今為止相對 ＝ *for the future* ）
   in the future 未來

道 歉 · 婉 拒 函 模 範 書 信

A. 道歉信（Letters of Apology）

1

First of all, we would like to *offer* our heartfelt *apology for* a great delay in replying to your letter of May 15. Upon receipt of your letter, we discussed your offer by *calling conferences* over and over again, but owing to the nature of the problem, decision was delayed notwithstanding our endeavor to bring the matter into early solution.

....

We again apologize for *our long silence* and hope you will give the matter your best consideration.

　　首先必須為答覆貴方5月15日來函拖延甚久，致上衷心的歉意。一接到來函，本公司就一再召集會議討論貴方的報價，但是由於問題的性質，儘管我方努力儘早解決此事，還是延遲做決定。

....

　　我方再次為久未回信道歉，希望貴方對此事做最佳的考慮。

B. 婉拒函 (Letters of Regret)

1

Thank you very much for your letter of May 22 advising us of a *tender for* electric machines. To our deep regret, however, our present position makes it impossible for us to *join the proposed tender*, which you will *cordially* note. We thank you again for your kindness and look forward to your *continued* favors and attention.

非常感謝貴方5月22日來函，通知本公司電氣機械的投標。然而，我方深感遺憾，以目前的處境，不可能參加貴方提議的投標，望諒察。再次感謝貴方的好意，並期待您繼續支持與關照。

➡ tender〔ˊtɛndɚ〕 *n.* 投標
➡ cordially〔ˊkɔrdʒəlɪ〕 *adv.* 熱心的；眞誠的

第15章
請託函
Letters of Favor

　　請託函在書信中佔著很重要的地位，無論在商務、社交上的應用範圍都極爲廣泛。因爲旨在請託他人，所以文體必須彬彬有禮，不要忘了最後再次提醒對方請託要件。

　　初次請託函與非初次請託函的表現方式不同，請特別注意。

請 託 函 必 備 例 句

A. 初次請託函（Letters to Strangers）

　　a)「貿然請求，深表惶恐……」的說法

1. Permit（Allow）me to write a　　　　　容我寫信懇求貴方…。
   request to you....

2. May we *respectfully* ask you
   to...?

   可否懇求貴方…?

3. Please allow us to write you to
   count on your kindness and leniency in regard to our wish for
   ....

   仰仗著貴方的親切與仁
   慈,容本公司冒昧寫信
   申訴有關…的願望。

   → *count on* 仰仗;依持
   → leniency〔'linjənsɪ〕*n*. 仁慈寬大

4. May we ask you if you could
   kindly...?

   請問您是否能好意…?

5. Would you *kindly* allow me to
   ask you to...?

   能否容許我懇求您…?

6. Permit me to *intrude on your
   busy time* by writing a request to
   you.

   在您忙碌時刻打擾,容
   我寫信做個要求。

   → intrude〔ɪn'trud〕*v*. 打擾;強使他人採納

7. We are really sorry to *trouble*
   you with such a request.

   用這種要求麻煩貴方,
   著實感到抱歉。

8. Please forgive me to *trouble* you
   with such a request.

   用這種要求麻煩貴方,
   敬請原諒。

9. I have a *great favor* to ask of
   you, which I hope you will be
   able to *accord* me.

   我想要求貴方幫個大忙,
   希望您能答允。

10. Allow me to write you to **count on** your kindness and courtesy to be **extended** to my wish to ....

仰仗著貴方的厚誼，容我寫信申述對…的願望。

11. In this writing, (First of all,) we **tender** our sincere compliments and would ask for your kindness and courtesy.

本函（首先）謹致本公司誠摯的問候，並請求您惠施厚誼。

12. We are writing this to **solicit** your kindness and **patronage** in regard to our wish to....

冒昧寫信懇請貴方好意資助有關本公司對…的願望。

13. In this writing, I would **count on** your kindness and courtesy.

本函想仰仗貴方的厚誼。

【說明】　以上所列的十三個例子，應該按當時的 situation（情況），判斷使用何者。

　　　count on one's courtesy and kindness 是「仰賴您的厚誼」。

　　　respectfully 是禮貌用字。　11. 讚美、禮節兼而有之。

---

b)「請原諒這冒然來信」的用法

1. Permit (Allow) me to write you to **state** that....

容我寫信向您陳述…。

2. I make bold to write you to
   state that....

   ➡ bold〔bold〕*adj.* 冒昧的；無禮的

   我冒昧寫信向您陳述…。

3. *Greetings*: we are....

   敬啓者：本公司…。

4. I have the honor of writing〔to〕
   you *in person* to state that....

   ➡ *in person* 親自

   很榮幸能親自寫信向您
   陳述…。

5. First of all, I *extend* my sincere
   compliments and would like to
   state that....

   首先，謹致誠摯的問候，
   並願意陳述…。

B. 非初次的請託函（Letters to Connections）

a) 感謝對方以往的厚愛並再度請託

1. First of all, we wish to thank
   you very much for your kind cooperation and *unfailing*（deep,
   gracious, utmost, *etc*.）*courtesy*
   extended to us during the past
   year.〔And again permit us to
   write you to ask for your special favor *in connection with*....〕
   At present, we....

   首先，對貴方於去年賜
   予我方親切的合作與不
   斷的（深切的、親切的、
   極度的…）禮遇，致上
   最高謝忱。〔並請再度
   允許我方寫信請求您在
   …方面特別關愛。〕目
   前，我方…。

   ➡ unfailing〔ʌn'felɪŋ〕*adj.* 無止境的；無例外的

2. First of all, we wish to express
   our heartiest thanks for your
   unfailing courtesy and patronage
   you have always **rendered** to our
   corporation. 〔May we ask you
   again if you could kindly **entertain our wish to**...?〕 This time,
   (At present, *etc*.) we....

   首先對貴方始終施予本
   公司的禮遇與惠顧，致
   上由衷謝忱。〔可否再
   度懇請貴方考慮我方對
   …的願望？〕這次（目
   前），我方…。

   ➡ patronage 〔′petrənɪdʒ, ′pæt-〕 *n*. 贊助；惠顧

3. **In this writing**, we **tender our
   sincere compliments** and express
   our heartiest thanks and appre-
   ciation for the **close** cooperation
   and generous patronage you have
   always rendered to our corporation. 〔And again permit us to
   write you to **solicit** your special favor and patronage.〕 This
   time, (At present, *etc*.) we....

   謹藉此函向您致上誠懇
   的問候並對貴方始終施
   予本公司的密切合作與
   慷慨惠顧，致上由衷謝
   忱。〔並請再度准許我
   方寫信懇請您特別支持
   與愛顧。〕這次（目前），
   我方…。

4. Greetings: **we hasten to write
   you** to have your courtesy and
   benevolence extended to us **in
   view of** our long-established
   business relations. This time,
   ....

   敬啓者：鑒於雙方長期
   的交易關係，本公司急
   函懇請貴方惠賜慈愛。
   這次，…。

   ➡ benevolence 〔bə′nɛvələns〕 *n*. 慈善；仁心

【說明】 3.最爲有禮，4.用於緊急情況下。〔 〕中的字省略無妨。

b）「敬請惠顧」「請多多指敎」的表達法（可以和A、B配合使用）。

1. Your best and kindest *attention* to this will be highly appreciated.

若蒙好意關照此事，將不勝感激。

2. We hope you will give this your kindest and best *consideration*.

敬請貴方好意考慮此事。

3. We trust our request will meet your prompt and kind *attention*.

相信貴方將好意儘速處理我方的請求。

4. We look forward to your best and kindest *consideration*.

期待您好意考慮之。

5. *Commending* the matter to your kind *consideration*,

請惠予考慮此事，

6. *Soliciting* your best and kindest consideration,

懇請貴方好意考慮。

7. We should be very grateful if you could....

若貴方能…，則不勝感激。

8. We shall be very glad if you are kind（good）enough to....

若蒙貴方好意…，則感幸甚。

9. We would *solicit* your favor and kindness *in this instance*.

懇請貴方對此事惠予支持。

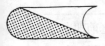　　請　託　函　須　知　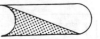

　　如同本章前面的敍述，委託函中初次與第二次、第三次請託時，寫法有所區別，須特別注意。

1. 「請～」的表達法
   a) Please....
   b) May we (I) ask you to...?
   c) Will you kindly...?
   d) You are kindly (cordially, respectfully) requested to....

【說明】　1. d) 是較正式莊重的用法，屬文體形式。
　　　　　2. request, require, demand 當中，以 request 最為有禮，require 和 demand 有「強行要求」的意味，尤以 demand 語氣最強。

---

2. 「若蒙…」的禮貌用法
   a) if you would **entertain our wish** to ～
   b) if you would **be good (kind) enough** to ～
   c) if you would **see your way to** accepting our request (wish) for (to + V)

3. 「敬致關係當事人」
   To whom it may concern, (一封信致多數關係人的形式，有如中文的敬啓者。)

4. 「期待您的指教」
   a) We look forward to your **guidance** and **attention**.
   b) I would solicit your **continued attention** and **patronage**. (用以表明繼續惠顧與指教。)

【說明】 若在 a) 的 your guidance and attention 之前加上 continued, 意思就和 b) 一樣, 表示「繼續」, 如以下例句:

We look forward to your **continued** guidance and attention.

5. write you 和 write to you → write you 是省略 to 的口語形式, 在美國廣為使用。和 Please write us at your convenience. (得便時請來信)是一樣的。但是, 英國仍用 write to you.

請 託 函 模 範 書 信

A. 請託函(Letters of Favor)

1

Prospects are bright for large demands for your new-type electric refrigerators now *on display* at the Commerce & Industry Hall, and would you send us five of them *on trial* ? When their sale proves *favorable*, we would like to place additional orders. So, we should be very grateful if you would also advise us of *possible price concessions* for our continued orders.

　　貴方現於工商會館展示的新型電冰箱景氣看好，需求量將很大，能否請您送來五台試銷？若試銷理想，我方將增加訂購。因此，若蒙貴方也告知後續訂單的可能減少的價錢，則感幸甚。

➡ concession〔kən'sεʃən〕*n.* 減讓；特許權

2

Greetings : we hasten to write you to ask for your cooperation and patronage *in our project to* open our business branch in your city. If, therefore, you would *be good enough to entertain our wish* and *see your way* to realizing our project, we would feel it a great honor and *spare no effort* to meet your high expectation.

敬啓者：本公司急函請求貴方合作支持在貴市開設分公司的計畫。因此若蒙您考慮我方意願，設法實行該計畫，我方將視爲無上光榮，並不遺餘力以求達到貴方厚望。

第16章
銷售函
Sales Letter

1. 初次銷售函　First-time Sales Letter

　　有人說 Every letter is a sales letter. 意思是所有信件都是動搖讀者的心意，使產生共鳴，以達到自己目的的手段（ instrument ）。更何況一封真正的 sales letter，當然要完全制伏對方的心思。sales letter 的至理名言是不要像義大利歌劇而採 **AIDA form**（ Attention-Interest-Desire-Action ）。首先以誘人的 Opening 吸引（**Attention-Winning**）對方，然後再 develop 這個 Opening，引起讀者興趣（**Interest**），最重要的還是使用一些鼓動購買慾（**Desire**）的文字──即強調 low price, fine quality, quick delivery, after-sales service, *etc.* 強而有力地引起 reader 採取購買的行動（**Action**）。

　　但是使用誇大言辭之餘要絕對小心，務必以誠懇、自然的方式增加**說服力**。美國人雖然喜用矯飾的文字寫 sales letter，但是我們的理想不是模仿美式銷售函，**modest、attractive、sincere** 的表達法（英式）才是上策。另外，為了讓 sales letter 走在時代前端，要避免陳腔濫調。不只是 sales letter，一般信件也要杜絕使用We take the liberty of …或We venture to offer …或May we beg …等古老用法（參考本章須知）。

　　還有一點極為重要的就是，**不寫長篇 sales letter**，簡短、動人的文章才是我們最終希望。長篇大論對商人是種負擔，也勢必遭受擱置的噩運。

　　總而言之，sales letter 寫作的重點歸結如下：

1. AIDA form
2. modest, attractive 英式寫法
3. 不用陳腔濫調
4. 禁絕長篇大論

初 次 銷 售 函 必 備 例 句

1. We are glad to have *the opportunity of introducing* to you our newly-developed product.

　　有機會為貴方介紹本公司新開發的產品，至感榮幸。

2. We are delighted to be able to introduce to you our *newest type* of product.

　　很高興能為貴方介紹本公司最新型的產品。

3. We are pleased to ***announce*** that
 ....

本公司樂於通知⋯。

4. Here is wonderful news for
 you! This time, we have ***developed*** a new type of car
 "COMET" even ***surpassing the
 level of*** a western production.

告訴您一個驚人的消息！
本公司這次已開發出新
型汽車「彗星」，其水
準甚至超越西方製品。

5. This is an age in which, more
 than ever before, customers insist on ***seeing goods before they
 buy***. This time, we have developed a new product....

這是一個顧客較以往更
堅持購買前先看貨的時
代。本公司這次已開發
出一種新產品⋯。

6. Great ***interest*** has been ***aroused***
 at the Trade Fair in London over
 our newest type of product ——
 STARLIT insulating material.
 Numerous enquiries have also
 followed thereafter.

在倫敦商展中，本公司
最新型的產品—星光牌
絕緣材料，引起廣泛的
興趣。其後更接獲無數
詢價函。

➡ insulate〔ˈɪnsjʊˌlet〕v. 使(電、熱、聲等)與外界絕緣

7. Harper & Grand Ltd. are delighted to be able to introduce
 a revolutionary family of office
 desks, THE STANDFIRM DESK
 RANGE.

哈普格蘭德有限公司樂
於介紹一系列革命性的
辦公桌—穩立書桌組合。

8. The prospects for its marketability is still unknown as it has
   just been *out on to the market*,
   but already *a rush of orders* are
   pouring in from abroad.

由於剛在市場上推出，
本產品的適銷性遠景尚
未明確，但已從國外湧
進大批訂單。

➡ marketability〔 ‚mɑrkɪtə'bɪlətɪ〕*n*. 適銷性

9. Why not *take advantage of* this
   opportunity to subscribe to our
   magazine now?

何不利用此一良機，現
在就訂閱本雜誌？

➡ subscribe〔səb'skraɪb〕*v*. 訂閱(雜誌、書籍)

10. Engaged in silk production for the
    past 50 years, we are sending a
    full range of silk products to
    various countries, winning a high
    popularity because of their *com-
    petitive prices and fine quality cou-
    pled with our sincere dealings*.

本公司過去五十年來從
事生產絲織品，向各國
出口各種絲織品，由於
價格具競爭力，品質優
良，再加上本公司誠實
的交易作風，故廣受歡
迎。

初次銷售函的結尾語

1. Please *just try and test* the
   merits of our new production,
   and also its own wonderful mo-
   bility！

敬請試試看本公司新產
品優越的性能，以及其
驚人的機動性！

2. We recommend you to try just once its own *unequalled merits* and *eminent mobility*.

其優點無可匹敵，又具有卓越的機動性，建議您不妨試一次看看。

3. Won't you come to our shop and check its merits and *unrivalled mobility*?

請來本店測試其優點和無可匹敵的機動性。

4. *Act now* —— post the enclosed card today!

立刻行動—今天就寄出所附的卡片。

5. *Simply* initial the enclosed form and mail it back!

只要在附表簽上姓名的第一個字母寄回卽可！

➡ initial〔ɪˈnɪʃəl〕*v.* 簽姓名的起首字母於

6. May we have good news from you.

敬待佳音。

7. We do hope you will be successful in *securing this offer*.

眞心希望貴方成功取得此報價。

8. We are sure that the goods will *meet your requirements*, and we look forward to your first order.

我方確信此批貨物必可滿足貴方要求，亟盼您的首次訂單。

9. If you think our offer meets your requirements, please let us have your order *at an early date*, as supplies are limited.

由於供貨有限，若貴方認爲本公司報價滿足需求，請早日發出訂單。

10. Upon your decision depends your
　　success. *Act now* and post that
　　card today.

是否成功有賴於您的決
定。請現在行動並於今
日將卡片寄出。

2. 勸誘函　Follow-up

　　一般 sales letter 都是同時發給多數的對象，稱爲 **circular**（**通函**,
只寫給特定公司的 sales letter 是 offer，不屬於現在所談的 sales
letter）。這種 circular 通常第一封是不會有反應的，還需要連續發出
兩次到三次的勸誘函。爲了不令人產生糾纏不休的厭惡感，**柔和地勸誘**
加上親切地追踪，非常重要。若直截了當地寫出「沒收到回信」，可能
激怒對方而產生反效果。例如：

　　As we have not yet received a reply from you, we *take the
liberty of* enquiring if you have now had the time to consider our offer.

　　由於還未收到您的回覆,想冒昧請問您是否有時間考慮我方的報價。

　　以上這種寫法咄咄逼人，表達方式也太陳腐，應該用下列寫法較爲
恰當：

1　Orders are now pouring in and stocks rapidly *running low*,
　　so we fear the time would be too late when you will *be disposed to* place an order.

　　目前訂單湧進而存貨迅速減少，故惟恐貴方想訂購時，已爲時太
晚。

　　➡ *run low* 減少
　　➡ *be disposed to* ～　想～

2 Now we are having a rush of orders and stocks rapidly decreasing; of course, we presume, you have *placing an order in mind*.

目前大批訂單湧進，存貨迅速減少；當然本公司假定貴方正考慮訂購。

➡ *place an order in mind* 考慮訂購

3 Orders are coming in one after another and stocks are fast decreasing. We fear you will miss the chance by *sitting on the fence*.

訂單接連湧進，存貨正迅速減少。我方擔心若貴方採觀望態度，將喪失良機。

➡ *sit on the fence* 觀望情勢

以上三個例子都是很成功的寫法，以柔和戰術加以勸誘是 sales letter 的重點。

勸 誘 函 必 備 例 句

1. *By now* you have received the catalog and a price list of our newly-developed product....

貴方此刻已經收到本公司新開發的產品…的目錄與價目表。

2. You have *probably* received the catalog and a price list of our newly-developed product....

貴方或許已收到本公司新開發的產品…的目錄和價目表。

3. By now you have probably *had a chance* to look over our catalog we sent you....

貴方此刻或許已經有機會看過本公司奉寄的目錄… 。

4. Have you had *an opportunity of* testing the sample of our new product which we sent you a few weeks ago? We hope so, because every report from those who have tested their samples confirms ....

貴方是否已有機會試用本公司數週前寄上的新產品樣品？但願如此，因為每位樣品試用者的報告都證實… 。

5. A new order-card, stamped ready for posting, is enclosed. *Fill it in now and save time later*.

隨函奉寄一張貼有郵票的訂購卡。請立即填妥以節省日後所花的時間。

6. You have probably intended to order shortly; if *we are right in thinking so, would you care to* place your order now?

貴方或許打算於近日內訂購；若本公司想法是對的，您願意現在下訂單嗎？

勸誘函的結尾語

1. Orders are pouring in and stocks are fast *running low*. We fear you will *miss the chance* by *sitting on the fence*.

訂單不斷湧入，而存貨迅速減少。我方擔心貴方會因採觀望態度而喪失良機。

2. A cabled reply would ensure immediate *dispatch from stock*.

以電報作覆可保證立即從存貨裝運。

3. You may be sure of our *immediate attention* to your order, which we look forward to receiving.

亟盼收到貴方訂單。一俟接獲，本公司必定立即處理。

4. Our whole experience is at your service and we hope you will make use of it.

本公司願以全部的經驗待命效勞，盼貴方加以利用。

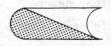 銷　售　函　須　知

1. 下列古老用法，請避免使用。

a) We *take the liberty of* introducing to you our new product.

b) We *venture to* offer our new product.

c) *May we beg* a moment of your valuable time to introduce our new product?

2. 以下列舉 Newsweek （新聞週刊）雜誌促銷的 sales letter。請加以分析比較，學習其巧妙的 AIDA Form。

ATTENTION—引人注目

Some recent polls show that the majority of all Newsweek readers are *highly educated* individuals; *leaders* in their fields and communities. *Like yourself* —— interested people, concerned people.

據最近一些民意調查顯示，大多數新聞週刊的讀者敎育水準都
很高；常是該領域和團體的領導人物。就像您一樣—感興趣又
關心（新聞）。

➡ poll〔pol〕*n.* 民意調查；投票

INTEREST—提起興趣

Newsweek is *the most quoted* newsweekly in the world.
A single issue covers a variety of *topics* that may
range from the armaments race to a new discovery in zy-
murgy. Newsweek's bureaus monitor world events 24
hours a day. Newsweek's *in-depth coverage* of politics,
industry, the arts, science, sports, and other news-
worthy areas offers *insights* that your daily paper cannot always provide.

新聞週刊是世上最廣受引用的新聞週刊。每一期都涵蓋多種話
題，範圍廣博，從軍備競賽到釀造學的新發現，應有盡有。新
聞週刊各部門，一天二十四小時監視著全世界發生的事件。取
材深入，範圍包括政治、工業、藝術、科學、體育、和其他有
新聞價值的領域，可提供您每天報紙永遠無法供給的洞察力。

➡ armaments〔'ɑrməmənts〕*n.*(*pl.*) 軍備
➡ zymurgy〔'zaɪmɝdʒɪ〕*n.* 釀造學

DESIRE—鼓動購買慾

Newsweek's *column pages* read like a *symposium of
name journalists and editors*. And only Newsweek
offers the *unique New Products and Processes, inval-
uable* reference material for businessmen.

新聞週刊的專欄讀起來如一本聞名的新聞記者及編輯的論文集。
唯有新聞週刊提供舉世獨一無二的「新產品與新方法」，是商
業人士無價的參考資料。

➡ symposium〔sɪmˈpozɪəm〕 *n.* 諸家論文集

ACTION—採取行動

Possibly you have been too busy to think about us and
the services we offer. Why not **take advantage of this
opportunity** to subscribe to Newsweek now?
Simply initial the enclosed form and **mail it back.**

或許您過於忙碌，無暇顧及我們及我們提供的服務。何不就利
用這次機會，現在訂閱新聞週刊呢？

只需於附表簽上姓名的起首字母，寄回即可。

銷 售 函 模 範 書 信

A. 銷售函（ Sales Letter ）

** 以下三篇宣傳素材相同，旨在宣傳「新產品」慧星新車，具有超
越進口車的性能和機動性，價格便宜又耐用，請仔細品味比較。

1

Our company is delighted to be able to introduce to
you our newest type of car **COMET** which may even
surpass the technical level of a Western production.
The prospects for its **marketability** are still unknown

as it has just been out on the market, but a rush of
orders is expected because of its *low price, superior
quality and durability*. We recommend you to try just
once its unequalled merits and eminent mobility.

能爲貴方介紹本公司新型汽車「慧星」，至感幸甚。該車技術水準
甚至超越西方製品。其可銷性遠景未可預知，因爲才剛在市場上推出，
但是由其價格低廉、品質優良、及其耐用性看來，訂單大批湧至是可以
預見的。其優點無可匹敵，又具有卓越的機動性，建議您不防試一次看看。

2

We are glad to have the opportunity of introducing to
you our up-to-date model car **COMET** which may even
surpass the technical level of a Western production.
Since the new product has just arrived on the market,
the prospects for its demand are still unknown, yet
we are certain of a rush of orders coming soon because of its *relatively low price, superior quality cou-
pled with its durability. Won't you come to our shop*
and *check its merits* and unrivalled mobility?

有機會爲貴方介紹本公司最新型汽車「慧星」，至感幸甚。該車技
術水準甚至超越西方製品。因爲新產品剛推出，其需求量的遠景仍然未

知，但是可以確定訂單不久將大批湧進，因為本車價錢相當低廉、品質優良、又很耐用。請到本店檢試其性能及無可匹敵的機動性。

3

Here is wonderful news for you! This time we have developed a new type of car **COMET** outdoing a Western product in quality by *concentrating the essence of our technical knowhow*. Though not yet sure of the prospects for its salability, we are convinced that it will find a great market because of its competitive price and unrivalled quality combined with its durability. *Please just try and test such merits and also its eminent mobility.*

　　告訴貴方絕佳的消息！這次本公司開發出一種新型汽車「慧星」，因為集中本公司技術的精華，品質遠勝過西方製品。雖然對其適銷性的遠景尚未確定，但本公司深信將會有廣大的市場，因為該車價格具有競爭性、品質無可匹敵、同時兼具有耐用性。請試看這些優點及其卓越的機動性。

B. 勸誘函 (Follow-Up)

1

By now you will have received our new price list giving details of the reduction in prices for all our dry-batteries, which came into effect on January 1st. Similar reductions were made in other markets and the result has so greatly exceeded our expectations that our stocks are rapidly decreasing. While we are producing at full speed, we may be unable *to keep pace with the exceptional demands*, and *a delay in despatch may soon become unavoidable*. You have probably intended to reorder shortly; *if you are thinking so*, would you care to place your order now? *A cabled reply would ensure immediate despatch from stock*.

　　此刻貴方將已接到本公司的新價目表，上面列有所有乾電池減價的詳情，於1月1日生效。在其他市場也有類似減價，結果遠超過我方所預期的，因而存貨迅速減少。雖然我方正以全速生產，但仍可能無法滿足額外需求，因此延遲出貨不久可能無法避免。您可能打算在近期內再訂貨；倘果然如此，您願意現在下訂單嗎？以電報作覆可保證卽期以存貨發送。

第17章
借貸關係
Debit & Credit

1.借記與借記通知　Debit & Debit Note

　　借記（ debit ）是簿記用語，意謂債務，記載於帳簿左邊。至於**借記通知**（ **Debit Note** ），就是借款的傳票。借記通知的收件人是**債務人**（ **debtor**，簡寫作 **Dr.** ），而發行人就是與收件人相對的，持有索取傳票面額權的債權人（ creditor ）。例如「 John Henry 1986 年 5 月 4 日向位於台北南京西路 5 號的三陽汽車公司，買進一台六十萬元的喜美汽車」時，其借記通知如下：

DEBIT NOTE

5 Nanking W. Rd.,
Taipei, April 5, 1986

```
Mr. John Henry
(address)
          Debited (or, Dr.) to the Sanyang Motor Co.
April 5    1 CIVIC AUTOMOBILE        $ 600,000.00
          Sanyang MOTOR  CO. LTD.
             Signed
```

```
             Manager
```

** 借記通知的發行日期即是購物的日期。此外請注意 Debited（*or,* Dr.）to 的介系詞要用 *to* 。

● **Debit 的用法**

「將一筆金額記入A帳戶的借方。」亦即由A的存款中扣去一筆金額

a)　to *debit* an amount *to A's account*

b)　to *debit* A's account *with an amount*

「貴方向本公司借款一千元。」

a)　We *debit* $1,000 *to (against) you.*

b)　You are *debited to us with* $1,000.

「貴方貸給本公司一千元。」

　　We *debit* $1,000 *for you.*

「請將一千元記入我方帳戶的借方。」亦即從我方存款扣去一千元。

　　Please *debit* my account *with* $1,000.

「貴方開立由 ABC 公司受款的一千元滙票，已承兌並記入您帳戶的借方。」

> Your draft for $1,000 in favor of Messrs. ABC was honored *to the debit* of your account.

借　記　必　備　例　句

A. 借記與借記通知（Debit & Debit Note）

1. There is a *debit balance* of $1,000 *on your book*.

   貴方帳簿上載有一千元借方餘額。

2. There is an outstanding balance of $1,000 *to your debit*.

   貴方尚有一千元餘額未付。

3. We have still a balance of $1,000 *to your debit*.

   同上。

4. The balance *still standing to your debit* amounts to $1,000.

   同上。

5. We have a balance of $1,000 still *standing to your debit*.

   同上。

6. The amount has been placed to the debit of your account.

   此金額已記入您借方帳戶。

7. Please debit our account with any expenses incurred on the case sent in error.

請將任何因誤送的情形所引起的費用，記入本公司借方帳戶。

8. We have *passed the amount to* your debit.

我方已將這筆金額記入貴公司的借方。

9. Acting upon instructions contained in your last letter, we *enclose D/N for cable expenses* in reference to this transaction, the amount of which please remit by sight draft on London at your convenience.

依據貴方前封來函中的指示，玆隨函奉寄與此次交易有關的電報費用之借記通知。請得便時以同額即期滙票寄到倫敦。

➡ D/N = *debit note* 借記通知；借項清單

10. The cost of a telegram to you, $20, we have charged to your account and *for which* we shall render you a D/N at the close of this deal.

拍給貴方電報的二十元費用，本公司已記在您的帳上，於本次交易終了時將對您提出借記通知。

借記與借記通知的結尾語

1. Please *honor the bill to* our debit.

請承兌本票，並記入本公司的借方。

2. We trust you will honor the draft on presentation to the debit of your account.

相信貴方於此滙票提示時會加以承兌，並記入貴方借方帳戶。

2. 貸記與貸記通知　Credit & Credit Note

貸記（ credit ）和借記一樣，都是簿記用語，意謂債權，記載於帳簿右側。**貸記通知**（ Credit Note ）則爲貸款傳票，發行人是債務人，收件人是**債權人**（ creditor ＝簡寫作 Cr. ）。「台北南京西路1號的新力貿易公司向紐約曼哈頓第五街35號的 New York Trading Co. Inc. 輸出三百個電器零件，誤將發票面額單價每個多記了二十分，總計多收了六十美元」時，其 credit note 如下：

CREDIT NOTE

　　　　　　　　　　　1 Nanking W. Rd.,
　　　　　　　　　　　Taipei, May 15, 1986

New York Trading Co. Inc.

35, Fifth St., Manhattan,

New York, USA.

　　Credited (Cr.) by Sunny Trading Co. Ltd.

　　Electric Parts ⋯⋯ per piece balance in your

　　　　　　　　favor ¢ 20

　　　　　　　total balance 　$60.00

　　　　　　　　　　　（¢ 20× 300 ）

　　SUNNY TRADING CO. LTD.

Signed
Manager

** 寫 Credit Note 時要用 by 這個介系詞，寫成 Credited (*or,* Cr.) by ～。

● Credit 的用法

「茲將一千元記入貴公司貸方帳戶。」
a) We *credit you* (your account) *with* $1,000.
b) We *credit* $1,000 *to you.*
c) We *place* $1,000 *to your credit* (to the credit of your account).
d) Your account is $1,000 *in credit.*

「您尚有一百元貸方餘額。」
a) There is a balance of $100 *to your credit.*
b) There is a balance of $100 *in your favor.*

貸 記 必 備 例 句

1. The drafts have been duly honored and the proceeds *placed to* your credit, *less* the telegraphic charge of $3.

滙票已按時承兌，茲將扣除三元電報費的營業額，記入貴公司貸方帳戶。

2. I have *placed* the amount *to* your credit.

    敝人已將此一款項記入您的貸方帳戶。

3. We have *credited* your account *with* $500.

    本公司已將五百元記入您的貸方帳戶。

4. We enclose a draft on the First Bank of your city, amounting to £1,000, *with which* please *credit our account* and acknowledge receipt.

    隨函奉寄一張貴市第一銀行一千英鎊的滙票，請將其記入本公司貸方帳戶，並確認收受。

5. The balance of $500 still *stands to* your credit.

    貴公司的貸方仍有五百元餘額。

6. Please be good enough to collect the amount and *credit to our account*.

    敬請徵收此一款項，並記入本公司貸方帳戶。

7. We are prepared to make you an allowance as you suggest which will cover the difference between steamship and railway rates. Please forward us your estimate of the same and we will immediately on receipt send you a *Credit Note for the amount*.

    我方準備按照您的建議，補貼汽船與鐵路運費的差額。煩請寄上估價單，一俟接獲，我方會即時奉寄差額的貸記通知。

8. Kindly send us a ***Credit Note for the shortage***. 　　煩請賜寄不足額的貸記通知。

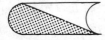 借 貸 關 係 須 知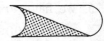

1. **Debit Note 和 Credit Note 的發行人規定**爲：

    Debit Note → 債權人

    Credit Note → 債務人

    乍看會有 Debit Note 是債務人發行的，而 Credit Note 是債權人發行的錯覺，其實正好相反千萬不要搞錯了。

2. 爲了清楚區分 Debit Note 和 Credit Note，通常前者用**紅紙**，後者用**藍紙**。

3. **Debit Note** 要用 Debited **to**（債權人）或 Dr．**to**（債權人）（to = against）。而 **Credit Note** 則用 Credit **by**（債務人）或 Cr．**by**（債務人）。

    也就是說，Debit to ～的 Debited 之上有收件人，意爲「收件人因～被記入借方」。另外，Credited by 的 Credited 之上有收件人，意爲「收件人經由～記入貸方」。

借　貸　關　係　模　範　書　信

A. 借記與借記通知（ Debit & Debit Note ）

1

We find on reference to your account that we have still standing to your debit a balance of £100.

有關貴方帳單，發現您的借方尚有本公司一百英鎊餘額未付。

2

Respecting your Debit Note No. 21 covering your out-lay for the telegrams to us concerning this order, we enclose First of Exchange Demand Draft on London, No. 28 for £1,000, *endorsed to your order*.

關於貴方因支付本訂單的電報費用，而開出編號 21 的借記通知，茲隨函奉寄指定讓渡給貴方而背書的，面額一千英鎊，第 28 號的倫敦即期滙票第一聯。

➡ outlay〔ˊaʊt,le〕*n.* 花費；開銷

➡ *endorsed to one's order* 以～為被背書人；指定讓渡給～人而背書

B. 貸記與貸記通知 (Credit & Credit Note)

1

We have the pleasure of informing you that, upon examination, we found the goods and invoice quite in order, and have, therefore, *credited your account with* $2,500.

本公司樂於通知貴方，您的貨品與發票，經查核無誤，因此，我方已將二千五百元記入您貸方帳戶。

2

We have duly credited your account with the amount on the invoice, *viz.*, £2,000 for which we will send you a cheque at the end of this month.

本公司已及時將二千元面額的發票，記入貴方貸方帳戶。將於本月底爲您奉寄等額支票。

第18章
海上保險
Marine Insurance

　　對外貿易時，貨物必須由海上運輸。在長期的航海途中，貨物因暴風雨或其他**海損（average）**而減少、損傷的可能性較陸上運輸大得多。因此，業者必須要對貨物投保。FOB、FAS、CF等交易方式下，由進口商投保，CIF則由出口商投保。

　　海損（海上損害）分**全損（Total Loss）**及**分損（Partial Loss）**，其中分損又可分為**共同海損（General Average）**及**單獨海損（Particular Average）**。

【說明】　海損（average）可從廣義與狹義兩方面來解釋，廣義地說，如同上面敘述的，包括全損和分損；狹義則指一部分貨物的損失。一般都採狹義的標準。

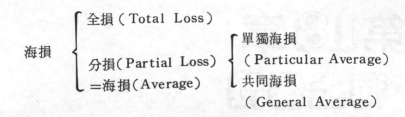

● 全損（Total Loss）

1.投保貨物眞正完全滅失；2.雖非完全滅失，但依規定可視爲全損；3.假定全損，例如船舶去向不明，已逾規定期限—— 以上三種情形，都視同全損，可領到賠償金額。

● 單獨海損（Particular Average）

是分損的一部分，指被保險物的一部分受到海上損害，且是不屬於共同海損的分損。因其責任完全由貨主單獨負擔，故名爲單獨海損。

● 共同海損（General Average）

雖然也是分損的一部分，但損失責任需共同負擔，故名爲共同海損。這種海損通常是因船舶或船貨在海上遇難，爲免發生危險或要減輕船體重量，而把船貨、一部分船具投棄（Jettison）海中，保全大部分貨物的海損。這是船長爲求共同利益而行的權宜之計，所以損害額應該由船主貨主共同負擔。

● 保險共分以下四種：

1.全損險（Total Loss Only, 簡稱 T.L.O.）

只有在貨物全部滅失時，保險業者（Insurance Agent, *or* Under-writer）才賠，保費（Premium）最低。

2.平安險或**單獨海損不賠險**（ Free from Particular Average，簡稱 **F.P.A.**）

賠償全損、共同海損，而不賠分損中的單獨海損。保費僅高於全損險，適用於煤、礦石等被海水浸濕也無關緊要的貨物。

3.單獨海損賠償險（ With Particular Average 或 With Average，簡稱 **W.P.A.** *or* **W.A.**）

一切全損、共同海損及單獨海損都要賠償，是保險範圍最廣的一種。

4.全險（ All Risks，簡稱 **A.R.**）

賠償有關運送貨物的所有危險（ Risks ）。但是，戰爭險（ War Risks ）、罷工、內亂、暴動險（ Strikes，Riots，Civil，Commotion Risks，簡稱 S.R.C.C. Risks）除外，須另定契約。保費最高，W.A. 次之。而 A.R. 和 W.A. 兩種是最常被使用的保險。

海 上 保 險 必 備 例 句

A. 申請投保（ Application for Insurance ）

1. We are desirous of *insuring a consignment* of cotton products ....

   本公司欲投保一批託售棉製品…。

2. We are desirous of *effecting (providing) an insurance on*〔物品〕*for*〔金額〕.

   本公司對〔物品〕欲投保〔金額〕。

3. Please *insure us on* (*insure for us*) the following : ...

請為本公司投保下列… 。

4. Please *cover us on* (*cover for us*) the goods detailed below :

請代本公司投保以下詳列的貨品 :

5. Please cover (insure) *us* 〔金額〕 *on* 〔物品〕.

請代本公司將〔物品〕投保〔金額〕。

6. Please cover (insure) for *us* 〔金額〕 *on* 〔物品〕.

請代本公司將〔物品〕投保〔金額〕。

7. Please *hold us covered on* the goods listed on the attached sheet.

請代本公司投保附表所列貨品。

8. We shall be glad if you will quote us a rate for marine *insurance* F.P.A. *on* a shipment of ....

如蒙貴方報知…貨物投保海上平安險的保險費率，則感幸甚。

➡ F.P.A. = *Free From Particular Average* 平安險 ; 單獨海損不賠險

9. Please insure (cover) us *on* *F.P.A. terms* for the amount of £ 5,000 *at* 30*p percent on* the shipment of ....

請代本公司以三十便士的百分比，投保總額五千英鎊的…貨物的平安險。

10. Please quote us by return your *lowest F.P.A. rate on* a shipment of cotton products valued at 〔金額〕 by...Line from Hongkong to London.

請接到信後立刻報知，由…航運公司從香港運到倫敦，〔金額〕的棉製品一批，其平安保險最低的投保費率。

11. We should be glad if you would cover us to the extent of £5,000 *at* 30*p percent on goods* in transit between Manchester and Capetown.

若蒙以三十便士的百分比投保本公司由曼徹斯特運往開普敦，總額五千英鎊的貨品，則感幸甚。

12. Will you please quote us a rate for the insurance *against All Risks* on a shipment of 50 cased CYCLES from Keelung to London, by vessel of the ～ Line ; value....

煩請報知，50箱價值…元的自行車，由～航運公司的船隻從基隆載往倫敦，投保全險的保險費率。

13. We shall be glad if you will *cover us against All Risks*, *warehouse to warehouse,* to the value cf $3,000, *on* the goods, from Keelung to San Francisco.

若蒙對本公司由基隆運往舊金山的貨物，投保三千元的倉至倉全險，則感幸甚。

➡ warehouse 〔'wɛr,haʊs〕 *n.* 倉庫；貨棧

14. Kindly let us know your rates of *premium for* an *insurance on* (goods).

煩請告知貴方對投保～貨物的保險費率。

➡ premium 〔'primɪəm〕 *n.* 保險費

15. We wish to have the goods covered *against All Risks.* The premium is to *be charged to* the consignees...together with all expenses of forwarding.

本公司欲將貨品投保全險。保險費連同所有運費，將由收貨人承付。

16. We shall have several shipments of CEMENT over the next six months to West African ports and shall be glad to know your lowest rates F.P.A.

本公司於未來六個月內將有數批水泥運往西非港口,並樂意得知貴方平安險的最低保險費率。

17. Kindly effect *insurance W. A. for* $18,000 *on* fruit, *say on* 300 boxes of oranges *on our account*, charging the premium in the A/S.

請用我方帳戶,對水果,例如三百箱柳丁投保一萬八千元單獨海損賠償,保險費記在銷貨清單上。

➡ A/S = *account sales* 銷貨清單

18. Please *insure for us*, *W. A.* £ 10,000 *on* Machinery, from London to Sydney.

請為本公司由倫敦運往雪梨的機械,投保一萬英鎊的單獨海損賠償。

申請投保的結尾語

1. We shall be pleased to have your early acknowledgement.

如獲貴方早日確認,則感幸甚。

2. We trust you will grant our claim *your usual consideration*.

相信貴方會如往常,考慮應允我方要求。

3. Please be good enough to *effect the above insurance* and let us have policy as early as possible.

煩請投保上述保險,並儘速給予我方保單。

➡ policy 〔ˈpɑləsɪ〕 *n.* 保險單

4. We await your definite order to cover.

恭候貴方正式的保單。

B. 保險公司的回覆 (Reply from Underwriter)

1. We thank you for your instructions to cover the *insurance on* your shipment of cotton products.

接獲貴方對棉製品船貨投保之指示，不勝感激。

2. We have received your letter instructing us to cover your shipment of cotton products.

貴方來函指示投保棉製品船貨，業已敬悉。

3. In reply to your letter of May 15, we are willing to accept *the insurance on all your shipments* of cotton products.

回覆貴方5月15日的來函，本公司願意接受您所有棉製品船貨的保險。

4. With regard to your letter of May 15, we are ready to *effect insurance against All Risks*, as requested, *charging* premium and freight *to* consignees.

關於貴方5月15日的來函，本公司已準備依所請投保全險，保費與運費由收貨人支付。

5. *Pursuant to* your instructions, we have insured your shipment of cotton products, *at the low rate* of 〔 premium〕, as per policy enclosed.

遵從貴方指示，本公司已照附寄保單的低廉〔保費〕費率，投保您的棉製品船貨。

6. We wish to advise having insured your shipment of cotton products, *up to value of* 〔 *sum* 〕.

本公司要通知貴方，已經將您的棉製品船貨投保，總值計〔金額〕。

7. We have pleasure in sending you *our rates on your merchandise* ...

本公司至為樂意為貴方奉寄貴商品…的保險費率。

8. Thank you for your enquiry concerning *our rates on your shipment* of cotton products.

感謝貴方查詢有關棉製商品…的保險費率。

9. In compliance with your directions, we have insured the goods provisionally *in the sum of* £ 2,000, at the rate of 2 percent.

依貴方指示，本公司已臨時為該貨品以百分之二的保險費率投保二千英鎊。

保險公司回覆的結尾語

1. We trust to be favored with a repetition of your commands.

相信貴方將不斷惠予訂購。

2. We thank you again for your command and look forward to your continued patronage and attention.

再度感謝貴方訂購，並盼您繼續愛顧關照。

3. We await your reply *in due course*.　恭候貴方適時作覆。

4. We trust that you will find *the terms offered satisfactory* and look forward to hearing from you.　相信貴方對我方提供的條件會感到滿意，並盼早獲回音。

5. This is an exceptionally low rate, and we trust you can *pass us the business*.　這次費率格外地低廉，相信貴方能惠賜這筆交易。

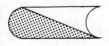 海　上　保　險　須　知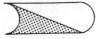

1. **單獨海損**　以個人責任爲前提的船舶或船貨發生的部分損傷。
   共同海損　以共同責任爲前提的船舶或船貨發生的部分損傷。

2. **warehouse to warehouse**　賠償從搬出出口地倉庫到搬入進口地倉庫爲止的一切危險，所以也包括 All Risks。

3. **保費（premium）占保險額的百分之幾**。英國是以每一百英鎊多少錢來計算的。£500 at 30p percent 以每一百英鎊三十便士的保險費率計算，金額五百英鎊的貨物，保險費共一百五十便士，即一點五英鎊。

4. **保險業者（Insurance Agent；Underwriter）**是基於委託人指示（Instruction）下，設定保費，賠償貨物。

5. **particular average** 就是 partial loss or damage caused to a ship or to a particular lot of goods（船舶或船貨的分損）。average 即 damage，由法語的 avarie 演變而來的。

6. 請記住以下的語句與用法。

premium〔ˊprimɪəm〕*n.* 保險費

rate〔ret〕*n.* 保險費率

W.A. With Average 單獨海損賠償

A.R. All Risks 全險

A.A.R. Against All Risk 擔保全險

F.P.A. Free of Particular Average 平安險；單獨海損不賠險

We have **effected**, for the account of A, the **insurance on** the goods **for** $ 10,000 at the rate of 10％ **with** the X Insurance Co.

　　本公司已用A的帳戶，向X保險公司，以百分之十的保險費率對貨品投保一萬元。

7. 投保金額比發票金額（Invoice Value）高出10％。也就是投保110％，即使全損也還保有10％的利潤（for 110％ of Invoice Value）。L/C 上常見以下用句：

Marine Insurance Policy or Certificate in duplicate covered with the American International Underwriters for 110％ of Invoice Value including W.A. and War Clauses.

　　以發票面額的百分之一百一十，由美國國際保險業者投保，包括單獨海損賠償與戰爭條款的一式兩份海運保單。

海 上 保 險 模 範 書 信

A. 致保險業者 (To Underwriter)

1

Will you please quote us for the insurance *against All Risks* on a shipment of 100 cases of CYCLES, from London to Malta, by s.s. " Atlantis " of the European Line ; value £ 7,500? The insurance is to be *warehouse to warehouse*, as from April 15.

　　茲有一百箱的自行車，總價七千五百英鎊，由歐洲航運公司的亞特蘭提斯號輪承運，從倫敦運往馬爾他。煩請貴方報知其全險價格。此保險將自4月15日開始，係倉至倉保險。

2

We confirm our cable instructions, as per copy enclosed , and shall be glad if you will cover us *accordingly*, against All Risks, warehouse to warehouse, to the value of £ 7,500, on 100 *cased CYCLES* from London to Malta, by s.s. " Atlantis " of the European Line. The *certificate* must be in our hands by the 17th of April at the latest, for presentation with the other documents to the bank *with which* a letter of credit has been *opened*. We shall be pleased to have your early acknowledgement.

茲確認電報指示，如附寄的副本所示，若蒙代爲投保一百箱的自行車，總價七千五百英鎊，由歐洲航運公司的亞特蘭提斯號輪承運，從倫敦運往馬爾他的倉至倉全險，則感幸甚。保險單至遲必須於4月17日前送達我方，以便與其他文件一併提出給信用狀開狀銀行。如早日得到貴方確認，則感幸甚。

B. 出口商→進口商（Exporter → Importer）

1

We have effected *for your account* the *insurance on these goods for* $5,000 at the rate of 10 percent *with* the Pacific Insurance Co.

本公司在太平洋保險公司以百分之十的保險費率，爲這批貨投保五千元，由貴方付款。

C. 保險業者囘函（ Reply from Underwriter ）

1

We thank you for your instructions to arrange the shipment of goods. We take it that you wish us to insure this cargo against the usual risks, *for the value of the goods plus freight*. Unless we hear from you *to the contrary*, we shall arrange this.

感謝貴方對安排船貨的指示。本公司認爲貴方希望對這批貨物，投保貨物加上運費總值的經常險。除非接到貴方相反的指示，我方將著手這樣安排。

貿易英語常用略字一覽表

—A—

@ at, to, from 單價，至，從

A.A. automatic approval 自動承認制度

A.A.R. against all risks 擔保全險
（海上保險術語）

A/C account 帳戶

A/D after date 出票後限期付款

Ad Val ad valorem 從價稅

A-1 A one 最高級的

A.R. all risks 一切險，與 A.A.R. 同

A/S account sales 寄銷清單

A/S at sight 即期的

Av avenue 大道；大街

—B—

B/- B/S bale(s) 包或綑
bag(s) 袋

bal balance 餘額；差額

B/D bank draft 銀行滙票

bd. ft. board foot 材積
木材的計量單位，厚度 1 英吋的木材
1 平方英呎即 $1'' \times 1' \times 1' = 1$ 材積(144″)

bdl(s) bundle(s) 束；包

bds breadth 寬度

B/E bill of exchange 滙票

bkt(s) basket(s) 籃；筐

B/L bill of lading 提單

BM(BFM) board foot measure 材積
與 bd. ft. 同

B/N boat note 交貨記錄，提貨人交
付租船的貨物收據

bot bottle 瓶

brl(s) barrel(s) 桶

B/S balance sheet 資產負債表

bsh bushel 蒲式耳

—C—

¢ cent 分

C/- case 箱（單數）

CF cost & freight 運費在內價

CFS container freight station
貨櫃集散場

CFT cubic feet 立方英尺

CIF cost, insurance & freight
運費、保險費在內價

CIF and C cost, insurance,
freight & commission 運費、
保險費、傭金在內價

C/N credit note 貸記通知

COM commission 傭金；代辦費

C/P charter party 租船契約(書)

C.Q.D. customary quick despatch 習慣快速裝卸

Cr. creditor 貸方；債權人

C/S cases 箱（複數）

C/S container ship 貨櫃船

CSK cask 桶

CTL constructive total loss
推定全損（海上保險術語）

CTN carton 紙箱

CWT(s) centum weight
（hundred weight）重量單位名，
（英）為 112 lb(磅)，(美)為 100 lb

CY　container yard　貨櫃碼頭

— D —

D/A　documents against acceptance
　　承兌交單

D/D　demand draft　即期滙票

D/D　documentary draft　跟單滙票

d/d　days after date　出票後～天付款

D/N　debit note　借記通知

D/O　delivery order　提貨單

doz　dozen　打

D/P　documents against payment
　　付款交單

Dr.　debtor　借方；債務人

d/s　days after sight　見票後～天付款

dup　duplicate　副本；一式兩份

DWT　deadweight tonnage　載重噸位

— E —

ED　export declaration　出口申請書；
　　出口申報單

E. & O.E.　errors & omissions
　　excepted　錯誤或遺漏不在此限；有
　　錯當查

ETA　estimated time of arrival
　　預計到達時間

ETD　estimated time of departure
　　預計啓程時間

— F —

FAS　free alongside ship　船邊交貨價

F.I.　free in　裝貨船方不負責，貨主負責

F.I.O.　free in and out　裝卸貨船方
　　均不負責

F/O　firm offer　確定報價

F.O.　free out　卸貨船方不負責

FOB　free on board　船上交貨價

FOR　free on rail　火車上交貨價

FOT　free on truck　卡車上交貨價

F.P.A.　free from particular
　　average　平安險；單獨海損不賠險

ft^2　square feet　平方英尺

— G —

G　gram(me)　公克、公分

G/A　general average　共同海損

GAL　gallon　加侖

gr.wt.　gross weight　毛重；總重量

G/T　gross tonnage　總噸數

— H , I —

hgd　hogshead　大桶，(美)可容納 63
　　加侖，(英)可容納 52.5 加侖

h.p.　horse power　馬力

IATA　International Air Transport
　　Association　國際航空運輸協會

ID　import declaration　進口申請
　　書；進口申報單

ID　identification　身分證

INC　incorporated　法人(公司)組
　　織的

inv.　invoice　發票

IOU　I owe you　借據

IQ　import quota　進口配額；進口限額

— K —

K karat 1.克拉（寶石的重量單位）
2.開（金的純度度量單位）
18-K gold 18K金＝18/24-K gold
（純金是 24K）

KG kilogram 公斤

KL kiloliter 公秉

KM kilometer 公里

— L —

lb(s) libra 磅（重量單位）

L/C letter of credit 信用狀

LCL less-than-container load 未滿
載貨櫃

L/G letter of guarantee 保證書

LIT liter 公升

L/T long ton 長噸（2,240 磅）

LTD. limited 有限責任的

— M —

M meter 公尺

m² square meter 平方公尺

m³ cubic meter 立方公尺

MAX maximum 最高限度；最高限價

m/d month after date 出票後～月
付款

Messrs. messieurs 公啓；公司

mi² square mile 平方英里

min minimum 最低限度；最低限價

min minute 分鐘

m/m millimeter 公釐

M/R mate's receipt 大副收據

M/S motor ship 輪船

M/T metric ton 公噸

M/V motor vessel 輪船

— N,O —

N.D. non-delivery 不交貨；提貨不着

N/P non-payment 拒付

N/R notice of readiness 備裝通知

n.wt. net weight 淨重

Ord. No. order number 訂單號碼

O/S on sale 廉售

oz onza(L) 盎絲

— P,Q —

P/A particular average 單獨海損

patt pattern 類型

pc(s) piece(s) 個

p.p. per proxy 經由代理

qlty. quality 品質

qr. quarter 四分之一

qty. quantity 數量

qy quay 碼頭

— S —

S/D sight draft 即期匯票

SHEX Sundays & holidays excepted
星期例假日除外

S/O shipping order 裝運單

sq. square 平方

sq.ft. square foot 平方英尺

sq. m.　square meter　平方公尺

sq. mi.　square mile　平方英里

S.R.C.C.　Risks strikes, riots, civil commotion Risks　罷工、暴動、內亂條款（海上保險術語）

s.s.　steamship　汽船

S/T　short ton　短噸（美，2,000磅）

— T , V —

TEU　twenty-foot equivalent unit　長20英呎縱橫等積車輛（貨櫃用語），長20英呎的貨櫃（通常以 $20' \times 8' \times 8'$ 的貨櫃車最多）

T.L.O.　total loss only　僅擔保全損險

T/R　trust receipt　信託收據

T.Q.　tale quale　現狀條件（運輸途中損害買方負擔）

T.T.　telegraphic transfer　電滙

T.T.　Buying　電滙買價

T.T.　Selling　電滙賣價

viz　namely　亦即

— W , Y —

W.A.　with average　單獨海損賠償（海上保險術語）

W/M　weight or measurement　重量或材積

W.P.A.　with particular average　單獨海損賠償　與W.A.同

W.R.　war risk　戰爭險（海上保險術語）

wt　weight　重量

W.W.D.　weather working days　晴天工作日

yd　yard　碼

說英文高手 與傳統會話教材有何不同？

1. 我們學了那麼多年的英語會語，為什麼還不會說？

我們所使用的教材不對。傳統實況會話教材，如去郵局、在機場、看醫生等，勉強背下來，哪有機會使用？不使用就會忘記。等到有一天到了郵局，早就忘了你所學的。

2.「說英文高手」這本書，和傳統的英語會話教材有何不同？

「說英文高手」這本書，以三句為一組，任何時候都可以說，可以對外國人說，也可以和中國人說，有時可自言自語說。例如：你幾乎天天都可以說：What a beautiful day it is! It's not too hot. It's not too cold. It's just right. 傳統的英語會話教材，都是以兩個人以上的對話為主，主角又是你，又是別人，當然記不下來。「說英文高手」的主角就是你，先從你天天可說的話開始。把你要說的話用英文表達出來，所以容易記下來。

3. 為什麼用「說英文高手」這本書，學了馬上就會說？

書中的教材，學起來有趣，一次說三句，不容易忘記。例如：你有很多機會可以對朋友說：Never give up. Never give in. Never say never.

4. 傳統會話教材目標不明確，一句句學，學了後面，忘了前面，一輩子記不起來。「說英文高手」目標明確，先從一次說三句開始，自我訓練以後，能夠隨時說六句以上，例如：你說的話，別人不相信，傳統會話只教你一句：I'm not kidding. 連這句話你都會忘掉。「說英文高手」教你一次說很多句：

I mean what I say.
I say what I mean.
I really mean it.

I'm not kidding you.
I'm not joking with you.
I'm telling you the truth.

你唸唸看，背這六句是不是比背一句容易呢？能夠一次說六句以上英文，你會有無比興奮的感覺，當說英文變成你的愛好的時候，你的目標就達成。

全省各大書局均售 ◉ 書180元 / 錄音帶四卷500元

✌「**說英文高手**」為劉毅老師最新創作，是學習出版公司轟動全國的暢銷新書。已被多所學校採用為會話教材。本書適合高中及大學使用，也適合自修。

本書另有錄音帶四捲，由美籍電台播音員錄音，
配合學習，效果更佳。

英文商業知識入門

編著 / 卓美玲

校訂 / 劉文欽・史濟蘭・葉淑霞

　　　　陳靜宜・林叙儀

　　　　Bruce S. Stewart

　　　　Kenyon T. Cotton

　　　　David Brotman

美編 / 曹馨元・許靜雯・邱招娣

打字 / 黃淑貞・賴秋燕・蘇淑玲

　　　　鄭梅芳・倪秀梅

校對 / 王淑珍・袁愛琴

學習出版，天天進步

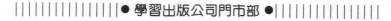

||||||||||||● 學習出版公司門市部 ●||||||||||||||

台北地區：台北市許昌街 10 號 2 樓 TEL：(02)2331-4060・2331-9209
台中地區：台中市綠川東街 32 號 8 樓 23 室
　　　　　TEL：(04)2223-2838

||||||||||||||||||||||||||||||||||||||||||||||||

英文商業知識入門

編　　著／卓 美 玲
發 行 所／學習出版有限公司　　　　　☎ (02) 2704-5525
郵 撥 帳 號／0512727-2 學習出版社帳戶
登 記 證／局版台業 2179 號
印 刷 所／裕強彩色印刷有限公司
台 北 門 市／台北市許昌街 10 號 2 F　　　☎ (02) 2331-4060・2331-9209
台 中 門 市／台中市綠川東街 32 號 8 F 23 室　☎ (04) 2223-2838
台灣總經銷／紅螞蟻圖書有限公司　　　　☎ (02) 2795-3656
美國總經銷／ Evergreen Book Store　　☎ (818) 2813622
本公司網址　www.learnbook.com.tw
電 子 郵 件　learnbook@learnbook.com.tw

　　　　售價：新台幣一百八十元正
　　　　2003 年 5 月 1 日一版六刷

ISBN 957-519-016-5